Scriptures for the Church Seasons

Lent 2012
Call Him Savior

John O. Gooch

A Lenten Study Based on the Revised Common Lectionary

Abingdon Press

A Lenten Study Based on the Revised Common Lectionary

CALL HIM SAVIOR
by John O. Gooch

Copyright © 2011 by Abingdon Press

ISBN-13: 9781426716256

Manufactured in the United States of America

11 12 13 14 15 16 17 18 19 20—10 9 8 7 6 5 4 3 2 1

Contents

ntroduction

In many ways, being a teenager in the 1950's was an idyllic time. I went through seventh and eighth grade, aware of the Korean War and the young men in our town who were fighting it; but as a youth, it did not touch me that closely.

High school was a time of playing basketball, participating in church youth groups and other church activities, starting to date, learning to drive, finding a job, putting money aside for college, and getting my license to preach—oh, yes, and going to school and learning things. It was a golden era for the church as well. Attendance was high, churches were growing, and money for missions came in freely.

As a general rule, though, we did not observe Lent. Oh, we all talked about "giving something up" for Lent, but it was more of a game than a religious exercise. We did observe Good Friday, and we participated in a community Friday serv-ice built around the Seven Last Words on the cross. School did not let out for that service, but those of us who volunteered to usher were excused from classes. Our youth group always volunteered eagerly to usher!

Today, we take Lent more seriously than when I was young. We have learned that it is a season in which we do more than give up chocolate. It is a time when we remember Jesus' journey to the cross and explore what it means to call Jesus our Savior. We recreate that journey with Scripture readings, sermons, hymns, and special music. We find ourselves growing in grace as we experience the richness of these practices.

A key part of living and passing on the faith is to tell the stories over and over. So we tell the stories, for example, of Moses lifting up the serpent in the wilderness and of Jesus predicting his own death with a reference to that story.

We remember the importance of baptism and being saved through water and the Spirit as we recall the story of Jesus' baptism and the story of Noah. We remember the power and the sacrifice of God's love through the incarnation of Jesus and the suffering and death on the cross. We celebrate the gift of salvation and new life in the Resurrection.

As we remember the stories and make them part of our own stories, we discover that we, too, are part of the story. The faith in which we live is not just something that happened "back then." It continues to happen in our lives as we remember and rehearse the old stories and see that we are part of them. We pass on the stories to the next generation, adding to the Scripture the meaning of the stories for us and for our children. The stories remind us that God saves us and gives us new life through Jesus Christ. During this season of Lent, may you discover what it means to CALL HIM SAVIOR.

y Water and the Spirit

Scriptures for Lent:
The First Sunday
Genesis 9:8-17
1 Peter 3:18-22
Mark 1:9-15

In the life of the confirmation class it was time to talk about baptism and what it means. Now, the congregation itself was young—only about 15 years old—and one of the blessings of that year's confirmation class was that the first three babies baptized in the life of the congregation were all members of the class.

The mother of one of them was a great storyteller, and she came to class that day and told the stories of those baptisms and what they meant to the church. She had pictures of funny clothes and hats on young mothers, at which the class all giggled. However, she also had a powerful story about the life of the church and what baptism meant in that life.

About that same time, the church was growing by leaps and bounds. There were lots of young families with small children and babies who needed to be baptized. We had an infant baptism at least once every month; and for several periods, we had one each week for three to five weeks in a row. It was an exciting time.

Every time we had a baptism, I had the opportunity to remind the congregation of the covenant that was being enacted between God and the baby being baptized and of the covenant that the congregation was making with the baby. They would promise to live lives that would be an example of faith to the child and to provide for him or her all that would be needed to grow in the faith and become a mature Christian. God was powerfully present in those baptisms.

Today's study is about God's mighty acts of salvation in and through water. The Old Testament lection, Genesis 9:8-17, is the conclusion of the story of Noah and the Flood and God's covenant with Noah. The Epistle passage, 1 Peter 3:18-22, refers back to Noah as God's saving act for eight people and the beginning of new life for the world. The Gospel passage, Mark 1:9-15, begins with Jesus' baptism.

This focus of chapter will be on baptism, the marvelous gift of water and the Spirit that God gave the church, and the salvation and renewal God offers through Jesus Christ.

THE YEAR OF THE FLOOD
GENESIS 9:8-17

It was 1993, and I was on a business trip through the Midwest. It had been a rainy spring and summer, and I knew all the rivers were up; but I did not worry too much. From Nashville to St. Louis was not much of a problem, although the Ohio was out of its banks at Paducah, Kentucky. The Mississippi River at St. Louis was well up the steps toward the Arch. West of St. Louis, the Missouri River was all over the bottoms and lapping at the edges of the highway.

In Iowa, the parking lot at the motel was sandbagged to keep the water out. Driving through Iowa and into Illinois was a nightmare. The heavens poured rain, and we wondered if the approaches to the bridge across the Mississippi would be underwater, as were all the fields on either side of the highway.

At every stop, we heard jokes about the plans for a cattle boat and questions such as "What's a cubit?" The story of Noah was fresh in everyone's mind.

In the story of Noah, the Flood was so big that it destroyed the whole world except for the people on the ark. When the Flood subsided, one of the first things Noah did was to build an altar and offer sacrifices of thanksgiving. After the sacrifice, Genesis 9:8-17 shows God's willingness to initiate a sacred covenant intended to protect all life from destruction. While the story initially provokes challenging questions about God's choice to destroy the world, it also illuminates God's power to save, reorder, and renew all creation and to make a promise never again to destroy the earth with the waters of a flood.

We all know about covenants in our daily lives. We sign them all the time. We have an agreement with the bank about the money we borrowed to buy a house or a car. The mortgage and the lien on the car are written covenants. We agree to pay the money back within a certain time at a certain rate of interest. Perhaps we live in a homeowner's association and have an agreement with our neighbors about certain rules and regulations. The benefits are services provided by the association. Maybe we get married and make certain promises to each other.

All such agreements are covenants. They are, basically, covenants between equals. Yes, the bank has more power than we do, but we are basically equals in the covenant. In the Scripture, covenants between God and God's people are not between equals. No one is equal to God. In the Bible, God initiates and establishes covenants. Such is the case with Noah.

Biblical covenants are gifts from God. They usually have three parts. First, there is God's action, or promise. Second, there is a clear expectation of what God's people will do in response. At Mount Sinai, for example, the covenant with Moses and the people of Israel was the Law, the Ten Commandments. The commandments described what God expected the people to do in their part of the relationship with God.

In today's lection, while the expectation is not as clearly stated as in the Ten Commandments, we see its beginnings in verses 4-7. In renewed creation, the assumption is that humanity will live better in the future than they did in the past. Then there is a sign or symbol that reminds both parties of the covenant. God set the bow in the heavens so that it would always remind not only God's people but God's own self (verse 16) of the promises and commitments in the covenant.

Through Noah and his family, God makes a covenant with the entire human race and with all the animals. Never again would floodwaters destroy all the earth. The covenant was intended to protect all forms of life from destruction. It was a sacred relationship between God and creation. God, who has the power to destroy evil and to renew all creation, has chosen to save and reestablish life according to God's original intent.

Genesis 9:1-7 echoes this intent with language that evokes that of Genesis 1:26-31. God blessed Noah and his family just as God blessed the original humans: "Be fruitful and multiply, and fill the earth" (9:1). God gave them provision and responsibility (verses 2-7). In effect, God restored order to creation in the covenant with Noah.

However, what does the covenant with Noah have to do with baptism? In baptism, we enter into a covenant initiated by God through Jesus Christ. We are reminded of God's mighty acts of salvation and welcomed into the long tradition of those acts.

We make promises of faithfulness to God and to the Christian faith, or our parents and other sponsors make them for us. The congregation enters into covenant with the baptized as they commit themselves to help the newly baptized member of the church to grow in faith and have the support of the community.

The sign of all those covenant agreements is the water of baptism. We hear again the themes we encounter in God's covenant with Noah—the themes of God's salvation and renewal.

What particularly challenges you or inspires you about God's covenant with Noah? What does it say to you about God and about God's relationship with humans and with all creation?

FROM NOAH TO BAPTISM
1 PETER 3:18-22

The Epistle reading for today elaborates on God's salvation and renewal in difficult times in the life of the early church. Within the somewhat tangled wording of 1 Peter 3:18-22, these verses about Christ's suffering, death, resurrection, and ascension are not only the hope and the example for Christians who are suffering, but also the basis for understanding the covenant of baptism.

One's baptism makes possible the "good conscience" (verse 21), which I take to mean something like the awareness of one's relationship with God through Jesus Christ. Baptism also is part of the claim on our lives through that relationship, which makes it possible for us to remain faithful, even in times of suffering. Martin Luther believed that during difficult times we could find strength by remembering our baptism: "When our sins and conscience oppress us, we strengthen ourselves and take comfort and say: Nevertheless I am baptized . . . it is promised me that I shall be saved and have eternal life."[1]

Verse 18 reminds us of the incredible paradoxes of salvation. Christ suffered once for all, as compared to the ongoing suffering of those to whom Peter was writing. Christ suffered as the righteous one for those who were unrighteous. Christ was "put to death in the flesh, but made alive in the spirit" (verse 18).

That last sentence requires a bit more thought. Dying in the flesh reminds us that the Incarnation was real. The Son of God became flesh, fully human. Some in the early church, even as early as this letter, apparently, said that Christ was not human but only appeared to be. This statement reminds us that he was truly human and truly died. However, he was raised, or resurrected, in the Spirit. Death was not the final word, but death was overcome by Jesus' resurrection.

A couple of questions I heard many times as a pastor were "What about all the people who lived before Jesus? Do they have a chance at salvation?" Verses 19-20 provide a possible answer to that question, even as they raise interesting questions of their own. What does this mean? When did Christ do this? What "spirits in prison"?

The text of verse 19 suggests that the spirits to whom Christ preached are those who were disobedient (in contrast to the obedience of Noah) and who died in the Flood. The emphasis on Noah and his "days" would tend to support this. The interpretation could also be expanded to include all those who lived and died before the time of Christ. Another interpretation is that between the time of his death on Friday afternoon and his resurrection on Sunday morning, Christ brought the good news to the wicked angels mentioned in Genesis 6:2.

When we were in Jerusalem the last time, a priest in the Syrian Orthodox Church told us of one of their traditional beliefs. He said that Jesus being raised from the dead was not a surprise—after all, he was God in the flesh. We should have expected that. The good news of the Resurrection, he said, was that when Christ rose from the dead, he brought Adam and Eve with him. Now, what that means, it seems to me, is that in dying and being raised, Christ not only overcame death, but also sin and the power of sin. That tradition is about the power of God to overcome sin.

Peter says that in the days of Noah, eight people were saved through water, and this salvation "prefigures," or looks forward to, baptism (1 Peter 3:21). This is a little confusing, since baptism says that God saves Christians *through* water; and Noah and his family seem to have been saved *from* water. The key, however, is that Noah and his family were saved from a godless environment. They were not saved "from the water" but "through water" from the evil around them. Just as in the case of Noah, the Flood was the death of an old world and the birth of a new, so baptism symbolizes the death of the old life and the birth of the new.

Baptism does more than remove dirt from the body. Christians are saved from evil through baptism as "an appeal to God for a good conscience, through the resurrection of Jesus Christ" (verse 21). This probably means something like a covenant response; being baptized is an act of commitment on the part of the believer that he or she will try to make the meaning of baptism real in his or her life. It implies that the baptized now has new virtues as a result of the relationship with God in Jesus Christ. Because baptism is an act of the community of faith, as well as an act of God, it is a call to live and work within the community and among its members.

The power of God that saves the baptized is shown in the resurrection and ascension of Jesus. There is nothing magical about the water; it is a symbol of the power of God and the mercy of God. So *conscience* also can mean the assurance by which we lay hold on our baptism in faith of the victory that Christ has won for us. We are not saved by baptism; we are saved by Christ. However, baptism is the sign of the covenant we are in because of Christ.

These verses remind us that baptism is a sacrament of salvation; it is a gift of God to the people of God. Those of us who are baptized are part of a long tradition of God's acts of salvation, stretching at least back to Noah. We are part of Christ's victory over sin and death. We rejoice in God's power and in the hope that we live in God and for God and that we will share in the glory of the Resurrection.

As you think about baptism, what does it mean to you? What could it mean to "live out your baptism" this Lenten season?

CHILDREN OF GOD
MARK 1:9-15

The year I moved from St. Louis to Nashville to begin a new career, I was lonely. My wife stayed behind in St. Louis to sell our house and wind up her job responsibilities before she joined me. On my birthday, I received a package from a couple of clergy friends in St. Louis. Inside the package was a framed poster. The poster said, "God danced the day you were born." I was glad to be remembered, and I knew the gift was an expression of love and support. However, I kept thinking, *I can't put this up. It sounds too arrogant. I'm not that special.*

After thinking about it for a week or so, I finally decided to hang it on the wall of my cubicle. Why? Because I decided I was that special, not because of anything I had done, but because God had made me God's child. It was another way of saying what the voice in today's Gospel lection said, "You are my Son, the Beloved; with you I am well pleased."

Baptism does that to us. We become children of God in a new way. We are all children of God in the sense that God created us. In baptism, however, we become children of God in the sense of being welcomed into the covenant, made a part of the community of faith, rejoicing in God's love for us. We recognize God's salvation and renewal given to all through Jesus Christ.

The baptism of John was not the same as Christian baptism. It was a baptism of repentance for the forgiveness of sins (Mark 1:4). Why did Jesus think it was necessary to be baptized by John? We do not know, of course, what was in Jesus' mind. Mark does not tell us. What we do know is that the details of his baptism proclaim his role as God's agent of salvation and renewal.

In verse 8, John the baptizer sets the stage for Jesus' baptism when he says, "I have baptized you with water; but he will baptize you with the Holy Spirit." A new outpouring of God's Holy Spirit was a sign of the end times when God would reign over a renewed creation (Joel 2:28-32; Acts 2:17-21). This view of Jesus sets the stage for two primary images that prefigure the identity of Jesus and his work.

As Jesus was coming out of the water, "the heavens [were] torn apart" (Mark 1:10). This is another apocalyptic image of the last times, when God would establish the Kingdom on earth as in heaven. It is an image that appears in Mark 15:38 to describe the tearing apart of the Temple curtain when Jesus died. The next image is the descent of the Spirit in the form of a dove, which echoes the biblical images of the Spirit hovering over the water in Genesis 1:2 and the dove in the story of Noah and the Flood in Genesis 8:8-12. It evokes the hope of a new creation.

Then came a voice from heaven, saying, "You are my Son, the Beloved; with you I am well pleased." The words affirmed to Jesus that he is the one who will bring salvation and renewal to all of humanity by proclaiming the good news of God's kingdom.

Immediately after Jesus heard the voice of God, the Spirit that descended on him "drove him out" into the wilderness to be "tempted" by Satan. The call to ministry must be tested.

In Mark's Gospel, this takes place in a single verse, without the long conversations between Jesus and Satan that Matthew and Luke include. Jesus was forced to think about just what being Messiah would mean. Was Messiah a fulfillment of the dream of political independence, driving the Romans out and setting up the kingdom of David again; or is it taking on the role of the suffering servant (Isaiah 52:13–53:12) who gave himself up for the life of his people?

The other image brought to mind by this simple statement is Israel wandering in the wilderness after their escape from Egypt. They were there for 40 years, being tested by God to see if they were faithful. This is another reminder of what it means to be God's chosen, whether Israel in the wilderness, Jesus in the wilderness, or you and me in the course of our daily lives. Are we willing to be faithful to God's call to be

Christians in all the little challenges of life?

I remember the morning after my home church had voted to recommend me for a license to preach, one of the leaders of the church said, "It must be wonderful to know you'll never have any problems again." I believe she meant well, but I also believe that her statement was a test of my call to preach.

Mark tells us that Jesus was with the wild beasts and angels ministered to him, which suggests that the enmity between humans and wild animals because of Adam's fall did not apply to Jesus. For Jesus, there is no danger from predators who would normally have been a danger. In the new day of salvation and hope, the wilderness will be transformed into paradise. The image also echoes the peaceable kingdom described in Isaiah 11:6-9. The angels are a sign of Jesus' relationship to God. The Son of God will be supported by divine assistance.

With the call of God tested and affirmed, Jesus went into Galilee and began to preach. On the one hand, he continued the message of John the Baptist, with a call to repent. On the other, he added a positive note: "Believe the good news."

The good news, of course, is what it is all about for us. Jesus' ministry makes the coming of salvation. The call to repentance is no longer about judgment and escaping from judgment, but preparation for the coming kingdom of God. Like Jesus, we receive the word that we are beloved children of God. We become part of the church, the community of faith; and we know that God is, indeed, pleased with us.

What does it mean to you to understand yourself as a beloved child of God? How does this understanding shape the way you live your daily life?

---

[1] From *The Large Catechism*, by Martin Luther, translated by F. Bente and W. H. T. Dau (*iclnet.org/pub/resources/text/wittenberg/luther/catechism/web/cat-13.html*).

Standing on the Promises

Scriptures for Lent:
The Second Sunday
Genesis 17:1-7, 15-16
Romans 4:13-25
Mark 8:31-38

My Dad was—and is —my hero. He worked full-time at the barrel factory in our little town and worked long hours at home keeping a large garden, repairing and painting buildings, milking the cow, feeding the hogs, and doing all the dozens of chores that go with maintaining a small farm.

He was a loyal member of the Masonic Lodge and served as its secretary for years. During the time of school integration in the 1950's, he was president of the school board and spent long hours helping the community move to integrate the schools. I never knew a time when he was not on the board at church, and he seldom missed a meeting.

Every day he was up early, doing the chores and then sitting down to breakfast and working out his lesson for the Sunday school class he taught. Much of the time that class was the senior high youth, of which I was a member. He was faithful to all the responsibilities that he took on because he believed in God and God's promises; and he taught me to be faithful. That is why he is my hero.

This week's passages are all about being faithful. At different times, *faithful* has different meanings. For Abraham (Genesis 17), it meant trusting specific promises that God made to him would come to reality. Paul used Abraham's faith to make the case for justification by faith, which includes all people as members of God's family. The Gospel passage is about Jesus being faithful to his role as Messiah, even though he knew he would suffer. He called the disciples to the same standard of faithfulness. All the lections are grounded in God's promises of relationship and life.

IF IT SOUNDS TOO GOOD TO BE TRUE ...
GENESIS 17:1-7, 15-16

If it sounds too good to be true, it probably is. If someone called you on the phone and said there was a prize waiting for you of $1,000,000, plus a new Mercedes, plus a lot of other stuff, what would be your first reaction? To be honest, I hope it would be like mine: "What's the catch? That's too good to be true." That is right. It cannot be true. There is a catch somewhere, usually one that will cost you money.

Abram had always listened to God and had always done what God wanted him to do. This time, however, it was too much. It sounded just too good to be true. Hang with me, and we will see what God said.

Abram and Sarai were old. Ninety-nine years for him, 90 years for her. God was coming around and giving them a new start with new responsibilities! What a message for those of us who are in retirement! Do not get comfortable. God is not finished with you yet!

The story begins with God identifying God's self. "I am God Almighty," which is the traditional translation of the Hebrew 'el shadday. God told Abram to "walk before [God], and be blameless" (verse 1). Being blameless—for example, faithful to the relationship—was not a prerequisite to the covenant. This was not a matter of "if you're really good, we'll make a covenant," but being faithful to God was required within the relationship. God gave the covenant freely. It was an act of grace, without any conditions. Once in the covenant, however, Abram was expected to be faithful to the relationship God had created.

Then God made a covenant with Abram and Sarai. Three introductions reveal each of these three parts of the covenant. "As for me" set out what God would do in the covenant. Then in the material not covered in the lection, there was Abram, "as for you" (verse 9) and then Sarai (verse 15), "as for Sarai." Each introduction led into an element of God's promise and of the covenant.

God said, "As for me, this is my covenant with you" (verse 4). Abram would be the ancestor of a "multitude of nations." Now, remember, this man was 99 years old and had one child by his wife's maid.

One sign of the covenant would be a name change. In the ancient world, a name said something about the character of a person. A change of name meant a change in character. So no longer would he be Abram ("exalted ancestor") but Abraham ("ancestor of a multitude"). Many nations and kings would be descended from Abraham. God would give them the land of Canaan, and God would "be their God" (verse 8). This would be an everlasting covenant between God on one side and Abraham and his descendants on the other. That was God's promise to Abraham.

The second part is what was expected of Abraham. One part of that expectation we have already seen: Abraham was to walk faithfully with God (verse 1). Further, God said, "As for you, you shall keep my covenant." In the verses "between" the two parts of this lection, God gave Abraham instructions for circumcision. All the males in Abraham's line would be circumcised when they were eight days old in order that the covenant "shall . . . be in your flesh an everlasting covenant" (verse 13). Circumcision was the sign for

CALL HIM SAVIOR

God's covenant with Abraham and his descendants.

"As for Sarai" signals that Sarai, too, would receive a name change (verse 15). She had been called Sarai, but now she would be called Sarah. The difference in the meaning of these names is not as clear as they are for Abraham, but the new name represented something different in her life.

The name *Sarah* means "princess" and relates to God's promise that "kings of peoples shall come from her" (verse 16). She had been barren, unable to conceive and bear children. When you are reading the Old Testament, and you run across a barren woman, watch out. God is getting ready to do something. That was true in Sarah's case. It was true for Rachel, for the mother of Samson, and for Hannah. In every case, the child to be born was a special part of God's plan—Isaac, Joseph, Samson, and Samuel. Sarah would have a son. She and Abraham together would be the ancestors of nations and kings.

Abraham was obviously comfortable in his relationship with God, because his reaction was about what one would expect. He "fell on his face and laughed." I can almost hear what Bill Cosby could do with this scene, Abraham listening to God and then cracking up. After all, the normal "rules" about fertility and childbearing were all being broken here. I mean, come on, God, you can't really do this, can you?

However, God did keep the covenant with Abraham and Sarah. What seemed too good to be true was good and true. Abraham and Sarah became ancestors of a multitude of nations. Isaac, whose name means "he laughs," was born.

When have you heard a promise that was too good to be true? What does the covenant with Abraham and Sarah say to you about God's promises? about your response to God's promises?

IT IS ALL IN THE FAMILY
ROMANS 4:13-25

Years ago, I was on a committee interviewing seminary students as part of the process toward their ordination. We had one young man who was trying to explain a theological point to us. He knew some of the right words, but he did not quite get the concept behind the words. The longer he talked, the more convoluted his thoughts became. We became increasingly confused about what he was trying to say. I was developing a major headache just trying to figure out what he was saying.

The young man knew he had not done well, so the next morning he came back with an illustration of what he was trying to say the day before. Unfortunately, his illustration only confused us more. The good news is that the next year, he had a much more mature and simpler explanation that made perfect sense.

Paul's letters are sometimes like that. Paul often dictated his letters, and they are full of asides, "bunny trails" that were laid down as he thought of something else in the middle of a sentence and blurted it out. His Letter to the Romans was a special case because he was not responding to specific problems in that church. He was introducing himself to the Roman church; and, because many of the Roman Christians had Jewish roots, he was being careful to explain justification by faith for Jews and Gentiles. Unfortunately, his arguments sometimes got a little complicated.

What Paul was trying to do was work out just what it means to be a descendant of Abraham. Obviously, the Gentile converts in his other churches were not physical descendants of Abraham, as the Jewish Christians were. In the verses just before this lection, Paul says that before he was circumcised, Abraham's faith "was reckoned to him as righteousness" (Romans 4:3). That is, faith came before circumcision. So it was Abraham's faith, not his works or his circumcision, that brought him justification.

Faith like Abraham's makes one a true descendant of Abraham (verses 11-12). The Law brings wrath (verse 15) because it defines sin. Without that definition, we would never know sin. Paul believed that the Law was inherently good and that violation of the Law is what incurs wrath.

Verses 16-17 are about faith, grace, and the promise of God for all people. God's covenant promises to Abraham are fulfilled for all people and are universally available to all who share the faith of Abraham, because he is the father of us all. Thus Paul included Jew and Gentile in the family of God.

Then Paul said something about the character of God. God is the one who gives life to the dead, which pagan gods cannot do, and calls into existence things that do not exist. The verse points to the power of God in creation and resurrection. In his commentary on this idea, N. T. Wright suggests that Paul's mention of God carries another overtone of meaning. When God brings a Gentile to faith, it is like a creation. When God brings a Jew to share the faith of Abraham, this is more like a life out of death, a renewal of covenant membership. Gentile and Jew, through faith, share the covenant promises of God.

With this in mind, Paul then analyzed Abraham's faith in verses 18-22. Faith is not a generic belief in an abstract "other." Most people in the United States, for example, believe in God. However, fewer than half of those who believe in God are involved in the life of a church or a synagogue. That is a kind of faith, but it does not mean much in real life.

Abraham's faith, Paul said, was not in a general god but in specific promises made to him by the God he had followed all his adult life. That is, specifically, he believed the promise of descendants in spite of the biological realities and his and Sarah's reproductive organs.

Abraham was "hoping against hope." He hoped in God's promise, even though realistically it seemed impossible. His body was as good as dead, but he believed God's promise of new life. He gave glory to God. He believed in God's power to do exactly what God had promised. This is the faith that was "reckoned to him as righteousness." This kind of faith, awakened in him by God's grace, is evidence of God's working in human lives for the salvation of the world. Faith is the sign of life, the gift of God. For us, being "justified by faith" does not mean that our faith earns us our salvation. Rather, it means that faith is a sign that God's grace has already saved us and brought us into the covenant, the family of Abraham.

Do you feel a headache coming on? Do not reach for the aspirin yet. We are almost through with Paul's complicated argument. Scripture says that Abraham's faith was that God could give life, which means more for the church than just the statement about Abraham. It also means faith that God raised Jesus Christ from the dead.

First, that means God gave life to Jesus who was "crucified, dead, and buried." Second, however, it means that God gives life to us as well, when we trust in God's promises of life. Faith is not a generalized thing in itself, but a faith in relationship to a God in whose promises we trust. For Paul, the primary object of faith is not Jesus Christ, but the God who raised Jesus from the dead.

The Resurrection means that God has for all time shown that Jesus is God's Son, the Messiah, the one in whom all God's promises come true. Believing that Jesus is Lord and that God raised him from the dead means having the same kind of faith as Abraham had. That faith, Paul said, is the only way we become members of Abraham's family.

The great climax of Paul's argument is composed of words that are familiar to all of us. Jesus "was handed over to death for our trespasses and was raised for our justification" (verse 25). This is another way of saying that the life-giving God in whom Abraham believed gave life to Jesus, in whom we believe and are saved. Jesus suffered and died for our sin. The cross is central to faith for Jewish and Gentile converts.

This statement reminds us of Isaiah 52:13–53:12, the song of the suffering servant. That passage in Isaiah also says that the servant, who died for Israel, is raised to new life. So the resurrection of Jesus is a way in which God intended to justify us. In a sense, the Resurrection is a declaration by God that we are justified and, in Paul's argument, find ourselves part of the family of Abraham in faith.

What challenges you or inspires you about Paul's understanding of faith? What does it mean to you to be included in God's promises?

BEING FAITHFUL IN TOUGH TIMES
MARK 8:31-38

In Mark 8:31-38, Peter challenges Jesus' understanding that "the Son of Man must undergo great suffering, and be rejected by the elders, the chief priests, and the scribes, and be killed, and after three days rise again" (verse 31). Peter's understanding of the role of the Messiah was not this one.

He may have understood the Messiah as one who would demonstrate glory and power. He did not fully understand what Jesus knew would happen, and he may well have argued with him out of love.

We can understand this argument. Why should anyone have to suffer? That is what we think when a friend or a family member is in incredible pain because of cancer or some terrible injury. *Why should anyone have to go through that?* we think. The same is true for mental or emotional suffering. In our world, with the advanced painkillers that we have, suffering can be relieved. For example, my body tends to create kidney stones, and they can be incredibly painful. I can remember more than once when I was grateful for painkillers so I did not have to suffer.

So we understand Peter, just in terms of thinking about suffering. Then we remember that Peter was protesting against the Son of Man suffering. When he heard Jesus say that he would be going up to Jerusalem and fall into the hands of the religious authorities and be killed, Peter was sure he had heard wrong. After all, in the verses just before this passage, Peter had said that Jesus is the Messiah. Surely the Messiah would not have to go through all that. Messiah would have the power to stop the suffering on his way to the throne of Israel.

As he does so often, Peter overreacted. He took Jesus aside and rebuked him. The verb for "rebuke" in Greek has been used already in Mark's Gospel for silencing demons. So this was brash of Peter to think that Jesus had a demon!

Even if Peter did not think that, in the culture of the day, a disciple talking like this to his teacher would have been a horrible breach of conduct. It is no wonder that Jesus answered him sharply.

Peter obviously thought that *Messiah* and *suffering* did not go together. Where Peter said Jesus was Messiah, Jesus himself used the term *Son of Man*. The designation also occurs in Daniel 7:13-14, which says, "one like a human being," or literally translated from the Aramaic, "one like a son of man." In Daniel, this is a glorious, heavenly figure who is given an eternal kingdom. In Mark, Jesus indicates that the Son of Man will suffer, be rejected, die, and rise again. Jesus' description stands in stark contrast to the heavenly authority described in Daniel.

It is a question of faithfulness. If one is loyal to the faith and to God, one will be saved. Faithfulness is, in part, about trusting in God to keep God's promises. The new thing in what Jesus said is that the Son of Man will actually suffer. The suffering of the Son of Man (who is also the Son of God) is involved in our salvation. Jesus suffered out of obedience to and faith in God.

Given the reality of Jesus' world as expressed in the execution of John the Baptist, in the cruelty of Herod Antipas, and the Roman procurator, it seems highly likely historically that Jesus would have predicted his own death in words like this.

Certainly Jesus would have tried to understand his suffering and death in terms of the coming of the Kingdom. His prayer in the garden of Gethsemane shows that he was willing to be faithful, even if faithfulness meant suffering and death. He must have felt that being obedient to what was set before him and faithful to God's promises would be enough and he would be vindicated in the end. We see this in the statement that after three days he would rise again. God's promise includes new life.

No wonder, then, that Jesus called Peter Satan. Not that Peter himself was demonic, but Jesus recognized in Peter's rebuke the kind of temptation that Satan laid before him in an attempt to test his faithfulness. The rebuke to Peter was a rebuke to Satan. Jesus was going to be faithful to the call of God and to the suffering that he knew was ahead of him.

After this episode, which must have been painful for everyone involved, Jesus called the crowd together. Usually, when Jesus wanted to teach the disciples, he withdrew from the crowd. Here he wanted everyone to hear about what it means to be a disciple. This again was about faithfulness. Even though Abraham was not mentioned by name, it is easy to imagine the example of Abraham's faithfulness in the minds of Jesus and those who heard him.

So what does it mean to be a disciple? A disciple must take up the cross, must be willing to lose his or her life, must not "be ashamed of" Jesus and his words (verses 34-38).

The promise offered for such faithfulness is life (verses 35-36).

It is not easy to be a disciple. It is a question of losing one's life for the sake of Jesus and the good news. Anyone who tries to save his life will lose it, and those who are willing to lose their lives for Jesus' sake will save them. So what does that mean for us? It means that it is not always easy to be faithful in our world.

We are disciples during times of loss, whether it means the death of a loved one, being laid off from our jobs, going through a divorce, or suffering from a life-threatening illness. We are disciples when we witness poverty, pain, and injustice. We are disciples when we question or affirm the values of our leaders.

The Messiah, God's anointed, was expected to establish God's realm in which all people would live according to God's ways of mercy and justice. To be a disciple means that we are willing to follow, to grow, to learn these ways, and to practice them daily—even in the midst of a world that contains great suffering, even though we may suffer, and even when times are tough. We take up our cross because we are faithful in our hope that God's promises of new life will be fulfilled.

What does it mean to you to "take up your cross"? to be faithful to God and to God's call in your life? to trust God's promise of life?

God's Wisdom and the World's Wisdom

Scriptures for Lent:
The Third Sunday
Exodus 20:1-17
1 Corinthians 1:18-25
John 2:13-22

In today's world, it seems that the important thing is to get ahead, no matter at whose expense. It also seems that ideology trumps everything else. If you just believe in the right way, that is, if you agree with me, then you are all right. If you do not, then it does not matter how conscientious you are, how carefully you think, or how much you try to do the right thing, you are just not acceptable. These attitudes often pass for worldly wisdom.

There is also what we call conventional wisdom. Conventional wisdom says that certain things will happen because that is the way the world is. We hear about this most often in terms of political races; but it is true in economics and in social relationships, too. We pay pollsters great sums of money to find out what the conventional wisdom is. We watch the cartoons about "gurus" on the mountaintop. Some poor soul has climbed all the way up this huge mountain to learn wisdom from the guru only to be disappointed because all the guru has to offer is more conventional wisdom.

Today's Scripture passages are about how God's wisdom reveals that the wisdom of the world is mere foolishness at the same time that the world thinks God's message is foolish. How is that for a mixed-up mess?

Here is how it will work. The Old Testament passage (Exodus 20:1-17) is based on a fugitive from justice (Moses) speaking for a group of slaves to the most powerful ruler in the known world (Ramesses the Great). Conventional wisdom would say, "No contest. Ramesses will win that one hands down." However, conventional wisdom does not take God into account. So, after the people were freed from slavery and led into the wilderness, God gave Moses a set of guidelines for establishing a different kind of society. God's wisdom is revealed in the Ten Commandments, which provide a radical way of structuring our lives.

The Epistle reading (1 Corinthians 1:18-25) goes right to the heart of today's theme. Paul contrasted the wisdom of the world/foolishness of God with the wisdom of God/ foolishness of the world. Using

Paul's categories, we will look at the idea of conventional wisdom as compared to God's wisdom.

Finally, the Gospel passage (John 2:13-22) is about Jesus protesting, in the name of God, the economic exploitation of the poor by those who were buying and selling in the Temple. He violently turned aside the conventional wisdom of making money, contrasting it with the need for a place committed to worship.

A NEW WAY OF LOOKING AT LIFE
EXODUS 20:1-17

In our Scripture, God begins by reminding the people of the mighty act of liberation in the Exodus from Egypt: "I am the LORD your God, who brought you out of the land of Egypt, out of the house of slavery" (Exodus 20:2). Egypt was a super-power, yet God chose a band of escaped slaves to be the recipients of the covenant! God's wisdom would be revealed in laws for life in covenant relationship with God and with one another.

The remaining section of the passage gives the Ten Commandments in which God told the people what was expected of them. The Ten Commandments are not just a set of rules; they are what it would take for these former slaves to become a nation.

The covenant with Israel was based on the conviction that the Exodus was God's work. So Israel was to have no other gods besides God. The second commandment told them not to make any idols. Ouch! We say all the time that

so-and-so is our "idol." The idol may be an athlete, a rock star, a politician, or a craving for more power or wealth or status. We even have a popular program called *American Idol.* For Israel, the command was clear. There could be no loyalty or idolizing of any god who did not save them from Egypt.

I can remember thinking that the third commandment meant that I should not use "bad words," and that is an acceptable understanding in terms of polite conversation. However, the commandment has a deeper meaning than that. It means to invoke God's name for purposes that do not fit with the character of God. For example, to oppress people of a different color or class or start a war with someone who has never harmed us and say that God approves would be using God's name for our own purposes. These would all be ways in which the God of the Exodus would be trivialized. God is not a means to an end that would be counter to the nature of God.

The fourth commandment calls for a positive action, to remember the seventh day as a holy time. To do so is to emulate God who rested from Creation on the seventh day. Notice that the command says nothing about worship. It is a command to separate from required activity, productivity, and rushing around. Just stop, be with God, reflect, and rest.

My preaching professor once told a story about meeting with his pastor/parish chair when he was pastor of a large church. The chair asked him why he was not taking his day off, his day of rest. He replied that he could not get all the work done in six days. He told us that he would never forget what the chair said next: "If you can't get it done in six days, we'll find someone who can." God commanded the people to take time out.

With this grounding in the relationship with God, the commandments go on to talk about the moral foundations for building a stable society out of a band of slaves. We will look at each of the six commandments separately, but keep in mind that they are one whole.

I used to tell my children, "The first rule of civilization is don't hit your father." I said it in jest, and they knew that; but there is also a good reason behind that saying. Honoring father and mother means more than just obeying or being subordinate. It means valuing the lives of parents and being open to their wisdom. For the people of Israel, it also meant hearing from them the stories of the Exodus faith.

The same is true for our families today. Christians remember the ancient stories of God's people as well as the life, death, and resurrection of Jesus the Christ. The stories are handed down from generation to generation in order to nurture our faith.

The commandment against murder is blunt and clear. Human life belongs to God and must be respected. Biblical faith draws a line against the taking of another life. Whether we are talking about blood feuds, drive-by shootings, or even capital punishment, the reality behind this commandment should make us stop and think.

Adultery means more than the narrow definition of sex with another person's spouse. It reminds us that sexuality is wonderful and dangerous. The wonder of sexuality is available in community only if it is practiced responsibly and respectfully. Countless loving relationships attest to the wonder of sexuality. However, sexuality is dangerous because of the pitfalls of acting on desires that are destructive of persons and of relations within the community. Nathaniel Hawthorne's novel *The Scarlet Letter* is a classic reminder of the destructive potential of sexuality.

Not stealing means, obviously, having respect for the property of another. However, I have to wonder if it does not mean more than that. A person needs the necessary food, shelter, clothing, and medical care in order to live a life of dignity.

When, for whatever reason or by whatever means, a society makes it impossible for a person to have those basic necessities, is the society stealing from that person? Is it stealing from children when thousands of them go to bed hungry every night? Is it stealing from a head of household when he or she cannot find work that pays enough to provide decent housing for the family? Is it stealing from a person to deny him or her a minimum standard of health care? of education for the children? There is more to this commandment than meets the eye.

The ninth commandment originally addressed legal practice. The courtroom must be a place where truth is told and where judges are free and independent to follow the truth. Remember that witnesses in courtrooms in our country swear to "tell the truth, the whole truth, and nothing but the truth, so help me God." That swearing is a direct reflection of this commandment. Over time, it came to refer to the practice of lying in general.

The prohibition of coveting is about the destructive power of desire—in this case desire that is acted on publicly. Notice that the prohibition is about economics, about property rights. At the heart of biblical faith is a concern for the rights of others, particularly of the poor. The prophets hammered on this over and over.

Thus the Ten Commandments reveal God's wisdom about the well-being of a community. This covenant gave the people of Israel the foundations for a just and moral society. The laws show God's wisdom not only for them but for the entire human community.

As you read and reflect on the Ten Commandments, which ones make the most sense to you? Which ones challenge you? Why?

TRUE POWER AND WISDOM
1 CORINTHIANS 1:18-25

For years, the church had been run by one family. They were farmers who had hundreds of acres of crops. They had family members in important positions in county government. They were directors at the bank and owned an insurance agency. They were also good citizens. They supported programs to advance the community, to pro-vide for children, and to help those who needed it in order to get by. They were loyal members of the church, filling two pews each week, singing in the choir, teaching Sunday school, and serving on the board. Whenever an important decision needed to be made, everyone else waited to see how the various members of this family would vote. They had status, power, and prestige.

In another church, in another town, a new family came to church and wanted to become members. The pastor called on them and began to ask about what they believed. It turned out that if they did not have the right ideas and the right beliefs, they would not be welcomed into the church. In another community, members of one of the churches often said to newcomers, "You need to come to our church. Anyone who is anyone in this town is a member here."

The Corinthian church had all those people in it, and Paul would deal with each of them in other parts of his letters. Here he was trying to set up a contrast between worldly power and the power of God, between worldly wisdom and God's wisdom. He did it by talking about wisdom and foolishness. Here is how the argument goes.

The "message about the cross" is shorthand for the act of salvation brought about by the life, death, resurrection, and ascension of Jesus Christ. "Cross" is a shorthand way of saying all that, but how is it foolishness?

The soldiers of the most powerful nation in the world crucified Jesus. Paul's message is that the carpenter from Nazareth that they crucified was even greater than the Empire! Who would not laugh at that? However, those who think the message is foolishness are perishing, that is, they are outside the salvation brought by Jesus. To those who are being saved, the word of the cross is the power of God.

So there is not only a contrast between wisdom and foolishness, but also between perishing and being saved. Both of those are ongoing processes that are happening at the same time. Paul set up his argument so that the Corinthians would see themselves as part of those who were being saved (just as we would, right?). "Being saved" is once-for-all as well as something that happens every day of our lives. Salvation happened once for all because of what God did in Jesus Christ. Salvation happens every day of our lives as we accept the amazing gift that God has given us and try to live into it.

Let us go back to wisdom and foolishness. Conventional wisdom can carry with it the aura of being right, of knowing what is going on, and knowing how things will come out. Conventional wisdom would have said that the followers of a crucified carpenter would never be able to stand against the power of Rome. Rome, after all, crucified that carpenter.

Conventional wisdom as Paul understood it does not take into account the wisdom and working of God. Conventional wisdom looks at power, status, economic influence, and other factors like these. Paul called such worldly wisdom foolishness that leads to perishing. The true wisdom, Paul said, the true power is found in the message of the cross, the death and resurrection of Jesus. God chose that foolishness to save the world. In so doing, God made all the wisdom of the world look like mere foolishness. God's foolishness is wiser than conventional wisdom. God's weakness is stronger than human strength.

Does that mean that learning and education are of no value? No, unless we choose to use learning as a status symbol, claiming that we are superior because of what we know. Conventional wisdom in our day says that education is a force that changes the world for the better. I believe that, in this case, conventional wisdom and God's wisdom are on the same track. Education leads to an increase in the opportunities for better jobs and a better future. God would surely think such wisdom is a good thing.

So why is Paul so dead set against wisdom? He was a learned rabbi, after all, and could argue eloquently. Paul was concerned that we not confuse salvation with having the right wisdom, thinking the proper way, or as saying something like, "I still think right doctrine will save me." That is the kind of wisdom to which Paul was opposed. He would put his learning at the service of God's wisdom, of proclaiming the message of Christ crucified to the entire world, no matter how foolish that might sound to others.

When in your life have you seen contrasts between the wisdom of God and the wisdom of the world? What difference might it make to use God's wisdom as the primary guiding force in your daily life?

JESUS' CHALLENGE
IN THE TEMPLE
JOHN 2:13-22

Talk about challenging conventional wisdom and entrenched power! In John's Gospel, at the beginning of his ministry, Jesus took on the religious establishment right at the heart of their power—the Temple itself. This episode is reported in all four Gospels, but the other three place it during the last week of Jesus' life (Matthew 21:12-13; Mark 11:15-19; Luke 19:45-48). John puts it here to highlight the challenge and threat of Jesus' ministry to the religious leadership.

Conventional wisdom says get everything you can for yourself, no matter who else may get hurt in the process. What was going on in the Temple was a mixed benefit. Pilgrims who came to Jerusalem from around the Mediterranean needed perfect animals for the sacrifice. It was hard to bring an animal from great distances and have it arrive in top condition. The people who were selling cattle, sheep, and doves were providing a service.

Of course, it was perfectly legitimate to charge a fee for their service, right? However, when a service is a monopoly, there is always the temptation to charge too much, whatever the traffic will bear. That is what conventional economic wisdom says.

The same was true for the moneychangers. Each male Jew was required to pay a Temple tax each year. The tax itself was a small amount, but it had to be paid in Tyrian currency. These were coins with no images on them, hence no violation of the second commandment. People coming from around the Roman world would have had a variety of coins, all of them probably with the image of the emperor or some other public figure. So like those who sold the animals, the moneychangers were providing a service.

When you fly to another country, one of the first things you see in the airport is the currency exchange. Of course, you pay a fee to have your dollars changed into the currency of the country you are visiting. That was what they were doing in the Temple. Again, abuses were likely to occur.

Jesus protested this system. Remember, this was an unknown rabbi from Galilee, come to the big city, and the first thing he did was start a riot in the Temple. The protest was on several levels.

First, Jesus was protesting the fact that the market was there at all. This was the Temple, the house of prayer. The commerce was being carried on in the outer courts, which were also used as a shortcut for people hurrying on other business. The outer courts were the only place where Gentiles could pray. Anyone who showed any interest in conversion to Judaism had to pray in a place filled with the noise of livestock and the shouts of commerce. Jesus' protest reminded everyone that this was the Father's house, not the cattle sale (John 2:16).

Second, something that John does not mention but that can be inferred from the background, the protest was against the economic exploitation of persons who had no other choice. The merchants could easily take advantage of the poor of the land, who were cheated out of what little cash they had so that they could worship properly. They could take advantage of the faithful who had come great distances by charging them exorbitant prices because they had no choice but to buy at the "approved" place. Taking advantage of strangers and of the poor are forbidden by the law of Moses.

So, in the name of God and of God's law, Jesus protested violently. John says he made a whip of cords and lay about him with it, driving the livestock out of the Temple (verse 15). Imagine a stampede meeting you as you came through the gates of the Temple! He overturned the tables of the moneychangers, sending coins rolling everywhere. The crowd may have gathered up all those coins and tucked them away! Jesus' message? "Stop making my Father's house a marketplace!" (verse 16).

Sadly, I suspect the merchants went right back to the same practices, getting every bit of cash they could out of everyone who came to the Temple as soon as Jesus was safely out of town. That is the way the world works. However, it is important to make the protest.

As I write this, protestors in Egypt have just overthrown the government that had been in the hands of President Hosni Mubarak for 30 years. Other crowds of protestors are working to the same end in Bahrain, Yemen, and Libya. One should not underestimate the power of a protest! Jesus' protest stood as a message to the religious leadership of his day as well as a message to all of us.

Naturally, the religious authorities wanted to know what authority Jesus had for what he had just done. They asked for a sign, and he gave them a strange answer: "Destroy this temple, and in three days I will raise it up" (verse 19). The authorities were amazed. "This temple has been under construction for forty-six years, and will you raise it up in three days?" (verse 20).

Of course, Jesus did not mean the literal Temple. He was talking about the Resurrection. Remember, he was raised from the dead on the third day; but no one understood this at the time. After the Resurrection, the disciples remembered this enigmatic saying; and then they understood (verse 22).

So what does that mean for us? Let me try a few ideas and see what you think. First, conventional wisdom about getting all we can, even at the expense of others, is not a good idea. It is not moral, and it is not being part of the community. Second, exploitation of the poor and the outsider is a violation of the law of Moses. It is a violation of the laws of community and will ultimately turn back on the exploiter.

Third, the protestor often is right in standing up against the conventional wisdom and challenging the right of those in power to exploit those who have no recourse. God's wisdom embraces good for all, and it may often challenge the wisdom of our world.

How do you see exploitation of the poor in your community? How might you engage the wisdom of God to make a difference?

God Loved So Much

It used to be that when I was watching football on Sunday afternoon, I would see at least one fan holding a large piece of cardboard with "John 3:16" written on it. I do not see those signs anymore. Does that mean they do not need to witness, or does it mean those fans have just given up? Most of the signs that I see when I watch television these days are about hate and fear. God hates this or that part of our society or our actions. It makes me long for the good old days and the John 3:16 signs.

People think about God in many ways, but the most dominant ways in our time seem to be that God is a God of judgment and a God of love. The God of judgment is what I call a "Santa Claus is coming to town" idea of God. You know, "he's makin' a list and checkin' it twice," and "he sees you when you're sleepin' "—as if God wanted to catch us doing something bad so we could be judged and punished.

One of the themes running through all three Scripture passages is that God gives forgiveness and salvation freely, but we have to be willing to accept that gift. The God of love is a John 3:16 God.

Today's Scripture readings settle the debate between judgment and love in a fairly definitive way. Numbers 21:4-9 begins with judgment. The Hebrews complained about the way they were being fed, so God sent serpents to bite and kill them. When the people repented, God sent a way of salvation. Looking at the bronze serpent could heal those who were bitten. Ephesians 2:1-10 reminds us that we are saved by God's free gift of grace, accepted in faith, and it is God's grace that leads us to a life of good works.

Finally, John 3:14-21 brings us back to where we started. God loves us. God's purpose through Christ is to save our world. Our belief leads to a life lived in God's presence in the present and for all eternity.

LOOK FOR LIFE
NUMBERS 21:4-9

When I was in college, the major indoor sport was complaining about the food in the dining hall. In a small church-related college, we all ate in the same cafeteria; and all of us ate the same food and complained about it the same way. We thought the food was monotonous. Tuesday lunch was usually a choice between chili and chicken noodle soup. Wednesday night was fried chicken. We knew what day it was by looking at the food in the cafeteria line. We ate the food, but we complained.

Moses had to deal with the same kinds of complaints. The Israelites complained about their "miserable food" (Numbers 21:5). There were no supermarkets along the way and not much in the way of water, either. The people were so tired of manna! "It was so good in Egypt," they said. "There we had vegetables and other good stuff. Of course, we were slaves, but at least we had decent food; and didn't have to eat the same miserable stuff at every meal!" Rather than celebrating salvation and looking for life, they complained against God and Moses.

However, the story suggests that you do not want to mess with God. Moses could not do much about the situation, but God could. The ultimate complaint was against God. After all, God took them out there into the wilderness. God provided the manna when there was not anything else to eat. Why couldn't God give them real food?

God responded by sending "poisonous serpents among the people, and they bit the people, so that many Israelites died" (verse 6). The word translated as "poisonous" or "fiery" comes from the Hebrew word *saraph*. The snakes were not just a natural phenomenon. They were divine agents, the source of punishment or potential healing.

In Isaiah 14:29, the seraph is a flying serpent. The seraphim were also involved in the call of Isaiah (Isaiah 6). They were around the throne of God and were associated with fire. They brought fire from the altar to cleanse Isaiah's lips and made him holy. These were the divine agents that God sent to punish Israel for murmuring. Their bite burned like fire, and it killed. The seraphim were agents of death but also of life and healing. The real point of the story is the healing property of the snake.

The people confessed their sin and asked Moses to intercede for them. "We should not have complained," they said. "We are guilty. Please intercede with the Lord for us." So Moses prayed, and God told him how to deal with the snakes. Notice that God did not take away the snakes. We cannot just pray to God and expect that all the troubles in the world will go away. It would be nice if we could pray and be rid of cancer, AIDS, poverty, hunger, and all the rest; but life does not work that way.

I am reminded of the story of the man who prayed fervently that God would take away hunger from the children of the world. God did indeed hear his prayer and answer it. God said, "What are you going to do about it?" The Israelites could not do anything about this plague of snakes, but God would tell Moses what to do.

God did not take away the snakes but did offer Moses a way of bringing salvation and healing from the snakebites. According to God's instructions, "Moses made a serpent of bronze, and put it upon a pole; and whenever a serpent bit someone, that person would look at the serpent of bronze and live" (Numbers 21:9). God offered a way to look for life and healing.

What we can learn from this is that the people had to do something. They had to look at the serpent of bronze in order to be healed. Self-indulgence on the part of the Israelites led to death. Faith in the power of God, represented by the bronze serpent, healed. Also it seems that Israel could never be so "terminally ill" that God could not heal them. Neither Israel nor the church is ever so far away from God that they cannot be redeemed.

I once had a parishioner who was convinced that her sins were so bad God could not forgive her. I kept telling her over and over that there was no sin God could not forgive if one were open to receive God's forgiveness.

God loves us and wants us to be God's people. When we get caught up in pettiness and whining, God can heal us and make us whole again. My wife calls that "praying for an attitude adjustment" or, if she is down, "an attitude transplant." God can always save us, but God also wants us to participate in the process. We have to "look at the serpent," to be open to God's grace, and cooperate with it.

What causes you to complain to others or to God? What do you think might happen if you choose to pray for and have faith in God's healing power for your perspectives and attitudes?

SAVED BY FAITH
EPHESIANS 2:1-10

In many families there is a "blessed" child and a child that never feels good enough to earn his or her parents' love. Some children feel that no matter how hard they try, they will never please their parents the way their sibling does without trying. However, that knowledge does not stop them from trying. In fact, they try even harder. The less successful they are in winning their parents' approval, the harder they try.

Now, the way these children feel does not necessarily mirror reality. Such children may be loved, but they do not recognize it. Certainly they do not realize that they do not have to earn love and approval. They continue to grit their teeth, try a little harder, and hope that someday they will win parental approval.

That family scenario also describes the way many people feel about their relationship with God. They know intellectually that God loves them, but that knowledge does not make it into their emotions and the way they order their lives. For years, John Wesley was one of those people. He knew about grace and salvation intellectually. He even preached it—so well that others were converted by his preaching. He was discouraged by the failure of his ministry in Georgia when he went to a meeting on Aldersgate Street in London. After the meeting, he recorded in his journal, "I felt I did trust in Christ, Christ alone, for salvation; and an assurance was given me, that He had taken away my sins, even mine, and saved me from the law of sin and death."[1] Like many of us, before this experience, he did not know that grace is like grits for breakfast in Southern restaurants. You do not have to order them. They just come! That is what today's Epistle reading is about.

Once again we hear the promise. Even though we are dead through sin, we can find new life in Christ. This is the gift of God, who is "rich in mercy" (Ephesians 2:4). The first seven verses are all one sentence in the Greek, and the God who is rich in mercy is the subject of the sentence. Sin is not the end of the story. Because of God's love, we have new life in Christ. Unfortunately, many people do not believe that God is rich in mercy. Instead, they believe in judgment and punishment, particularly for those who do not believe as they believe.

In verses 5-7, the language about being made alive with Christ and being raised up with him would, I think, remind the first readers of their baptism. In the early days of the church, persons being baptized understood the ritual as a symbolic dying with Christ and then being raised up with Christ. Paul says that the new convert is seated in the heavenly places in Christ Jesus (verse 6). This does not mean that the convert has somehow died and is in heaven.

No, this is more than a promise of future life. It is something that happens immediately after conversion and baptism, in this life. Life in Christ is eternal life in this world and in the next.

In the church today baptism is still a sign of being made alive in Christ because of "the immeasurable riches" of God's grace in Christ Jesus (verse 7). What happens in baptism is a gift of God's grace that welcomes the newly baptized person into the heart of God's love and into the community of God's people. We, too, enter into that new life in Christ and experience the joy and wonder of eternal life.

Paul said that we have been saved by faith (verses 8-9). This reminds us of what happened to Israel in the wilderness. God (acting through Moses) provided a means by which Israel might be saved from death because of the plague of snakes. Life was God's gift, and the people of Israel had to look at the bronze serpent to be healed. They had to have enough faith to do that.

So it is with us. God's grace is free to us. We do not have to earn it. We do not have to be "good enough." We just have to have faith enough to believe that God does love us and saves us from sin and death. We are not saved by that faith. We are saved by God's grace through faith. However, without faith we would not be saved. God loves us, reaches out to us, and calls us to be God's people. All we have to do is respond in faith and believe that what God says is true; but, oh, how hard that is for some of us!

Then we are called to live a life that reflects the grace of God to those around us. Verse 10 says, "We are what (God) has made us, created in Christ Jesus for good works." Good works do not save us, but they are acts of thanksgiving for our salvation. We do good to others because we know the love of God and want to share it with the world.

One way we share it is to do good to others. Let us put it another way. We can never be good enough, can never do enough good, or score enough "spiritual merit badges" to earn our salvation. We are saved only by the grace of God in Christ Jesus. However, we will not long hold on to our salvation if we do not live it out in the world. Doing good to others is an expression of thanksgiving and a witness to others of the love of God.

Have you ever felt as though you needed to "earn" love? What difference does it make to you to know that God's love is a gift and that you do not have to earn it?

GOD LOVES YOU
JOHN 3:14-21

For almost all my adult life, I have said that I *live* in the Gospel of John. I read and preach from the Synoptic Gospels (Matthew, Mark, and Luke) because they are important sources for faith and life; but when I most need a word from the Lord, I turn to John. Today's lection is one of the most powerful reasons why this is true for me.

The passage begins mid-paragraph with the reminder about Moses lifting up the serpent in the wilderness. What is the point of the serpent in this conversation? Moses "lifted up" the serpent, put it on a pole, and elevated it above the camp so all the Israelites could see it. Just so, Jesus said, the Son of Man must be lifted up. This is a clear reference to the cross and its saving power. However, we need to add details from other parts of John's Gospel that give this sentence even more power.

Jesus talked not only about being lifted up but about his "hour." This "hour" was the "right time" in the divine plan. The lifting up of Jesus on the cross was part of a larger event. The "hour," the act of salvation was not just the cross. It included the cross, but it also included the Resurrection and the Ascension. All three of these together make up the salvation event for this Gospel.

The hymn "Jesus Keep Me Near the Cross" communicates an important truth, but the writer of John would say that we do not want to stay too near the cross for too long. We want to move on to the empty tomb, the Resurrection, and the return of Jesus to the Father.

The point of Jesus' being lifted up is the same point as Moses lifting up the serpent. It is a sign of salvation. Just as the Israelites had to have the faith to look at the serpent to be healed, so "whoever believes" in the Son of Man may have eternal life. Again, we need to bring in an idea from other parts of the Gospel. The writer of John believed in the last day, the judgment, and eternal life after death. The word *eternal* indicates life lived in the unending presence of God. It is a life that begins in the present when one comes in contact with Jesus. That is, in fact, what the rest of the verses in today's study are all about.

The key to this passage, as to the whole Gospel, is found in verse 16: "God so loved the world." We all know this verse. When we were children in Sunday school, maybe even in youth group, and we had to recite a Bible verse from memory, we all hoped to be first so we could say John 3:16 and not have to scratch our heads to come up with another verse.

This is, in fact, the key to all life. God loved the world. God loved the world so much that he gave his only Son. This giving was the Incarnation, the point at which the Eternal Word of God, featured in John 1, became flesh, became what we are, for our salvation. This was God's gift.

Now here is the strange and wonderful thing about this verse. The word *world* is often used in this Gospel to mean everything and everyone who is opposed to Jesus. If that is what it means here (and it almost certainly is), then God sent the Son to save God's enemies! That is grace! The purpose of the Incarnation was and is that whoever believes in Jesus should have eternal life.

Note also that in John 3:16, there comes a note of judgment. Whoever believes in Jesus will not perish but will have eternal life. The implication is that whoever does not believe in Jesus will perish. God gives us a choice. We can believe or not, but our choice will

have implications that stretch from this moment to eternity.

One of the most fascinating things about a political campaign is all the times that the candidate puts his or her foot in his or her mouth and then has to send a spokesman out to explain what the candidate meant. Verse 17 is not quite a foot-in-the-mouth statement, but it is an explanation that elaborates on verse 16. God did not send the Son to *condemn* the world but to *save* it.

There was a period in the history of the church when the dominant image of Jesus Christ was as the heavenly judge. We have all those great paintings of the Last Judgment with Christ in the center of the painting. In the bottom half of the painting are the great majority of humans who are being cast down to hell, already tormented by demons. In the upper half are those few who are being saved, lifted up to heaven by angels, and the angels were not being overworked!

There are Christians even today who hold that as the dominant image of the relationship of Christ to the world. The Gospel writer says that is not what God intended in the Incarnation. Judgment is involved in the Incarnation, but it is a judgment that humans put on themselves. It is a question of belief. Do you believe that Jesus is indeed the Son of God come in the flesh to save the world? That is the whole substance of the judgment right there for John's Gospel.

The Gospel writer used another image to make the same point. The judgment is that light came into the world and people preferred the darkness. Wow! We can all relate to that. We have all, at one time or other, done something we would just as soon not have anyone else know about. Right? If there were a spotlight on our lives, we would try to run out of the spotlight on that issue. Keep that one hidden in the dark, so we do not have to think about it, or other people do not have to know about it.

Think about all the scenes in movies and cartoons about prison breaks where the escapees are trying to avoid the spotlight, which keeps chasing after them. The writer of John did not say anything about the inexorable pursuing spotlight. Instead, he said that light has come into the world in Jesus Christ. We judge ourselves by whether we come to that light. If we would prefer to stay in darkness, that is our choice; but we then have to live with the consequences. If we go to the light with our sin and brokenness, however, we find ourselves forgiven and healed.

Last Sunday, in my adult Sunday school class, we were talking about the Crucifixion and what it means. Someone brought up the story he had heard about Jesus standing outside of heaven, not going in. Finally someone worked up the courage to ask him why he was not in heaven, in the full glory of his divine being. Jesus' answer? "I'm waiting for Judas." That makes the point, I think, that all sin can be forgiven. It is only when we refuse to ask for forgiveness and new life that the judgment we make on ourselves has eternal consequences.

So this passage tells us about love and light. It is about what God gives to us and what God calls for from us. Do we believe that the Eternal Word entered into our world and became flesh in the person of Jesus of Nazareth? Do we believe God sent the Son into the world for all? Are we willing to come to that light and embrace that love? If so, we are promised life in the unending presence of God.

What does it mean to you to say, "For God so loved the world?" What difference does this reality make in your day-to-day life?

---

[1] From *The Journal of the Rev. John Wesley*, Vol. 1 (Epworth Press); page 476.

$\mathcal{F}$resh Starts in Faith

Scriptures for Lent:
The Fifth Sunday
Jeremiah 31:31-34
Hebrews 5:5-10
John 12:20-33

I was a teenager in the 1950's. Faith seemed so easy then. When I was in high school, I went to church camp every summer. We were inspired and challenged, and we learned a lot about the Bible and faith. I was fortunate enough to be able to attend sub-district, district, conference, and national youth events; and I was inspired by all of them. I was active in our church and the youth group and loved singing hymns and feeling close to God.

Then came college and seminary and learning in depth about the Bible and church history. Faith suddenly became more complicated. On the one hand, I was thrilled to learn so much. On the other hand, the old simple faith did not seem quite enough any more.

Then I got out into the world and ran into hard questions: race relations, war, economic policies, and all the issues of daily life facing my parishioners. Many times I looked at my faith, found something missing, and searched anew for faith and meaning.

Faith is like that for most of us. What was satisfactory to us when we were younger is no longer enough today. We continually start over or rework our understanding of faith. Today's readings are tools we could use in that process.

Jeremiah 31:31-34 is about fresh starts and new ways in which God chooses to relate to us when our circumstances change. Hebrews 5:5-10 reminds us that what was powerful for Aaron as high priest is overshadowed by what is powerful in Jesus Christ. John 12:20-33 reminds us, once again, that the saving event God worked out in the crucifixion, resurrection, and ascension of Jesus is the foundation for our faith at every stage of our faith development.

STARTING OVER
JEREMIAH 31:31-34

We all like the idea of a fresh start, which is why New Year's resolutions are so popular. We look at the new year, with all its promise and hope, and vow that this year things are going to be different. We are going to lose those ten pounds, we are going to be a better friend, we are going to—well, you know all the things you put in resolutions. On New Year's Day, anything seems possible. We are filled with confidence and hope. Of course, by January 10, we have already broken some of those resolutions. We were a little too confident, perhaps.

Maybe we gave up drinking soft drinks for Lent and then drank a dozen cans on Easter Sunday. We did not give it up; we just postponed it. More positively, we take on a new spiritual discipline for Lent and actually practice it for three or four days! It is almost as if we sang the old gospel hymn, "I'll go where you want me to go, dear Lord, o'er mountain or plain or sea" and then "if it doesn't rain on Sunday, I'll try to get to church."

The prophet Jeremiah looked back on the long history of his people, from the time of Moses to his day, and saw a long chain of broken promises. Israel had time and time again been faithless to their covenant commitments. Over and over Israel had promised to be faithful, yet they broke their promises almost before they were made.

The Bible names two major causes for the breaking of the covenant, both of which sound familiar to us today. The first was what the prophets called "chasing after other gods," that is, worshiping the gods of other nations, instead of worshiping YHWH alone. We do not worship Baal or Astarte; but we do commit ourselves to success, wealth, power, and other secular "gods" over and above the God of our faith.

The second way in which Israel broke the covenant was the economic exploitation of the poor by the wealthy. The prophets proclaimed the will of God for justice, compassion, and caring for those who were not able to care for themselves. For example, Amos 5:24 says, "Let justice roll down like waters." Jeremiah 22:1-9 called the king to justice and righteousness and threatened punishment if the king did not obey.

The words of Jeremiah that make up today's reading reflect the brokenness of the covenant relationship between Israel and God. Jeremiah reminded the people of how, again and again, the judgment of God had come to Israel because of this. The prophets blamed the overthrow of the northern kingdom of Israel directly on the economic exploitation of the poor and the worship of other gods, for example. He stressed that the brokenness of the covenant went back to the beginning of the covenant relationship with the nation after the Exodus from Egypt (11:7-8).

However, Jeremiah says that there would be a fresh start. The new covenant that God would make with God's people would not be like the old covenant that they broke so easily. This would not be an external matter of rules and obedience to rules. Rather, it would be an interior change—a new heart and a new spirit. God would write this covenant on the hearts of the people rather than on tablets of stone. To me, this means that God would so affect human hearts that people could—and will—keep the requirements of the covenant. That is what Saint Augustine called "co-operating grace," the aspect of God's grace that allows us to work with God to do what God wants.

Jeremiah also says that the future would be different from the past. In the past, the people had been disobedient and wandered away from God, which led to judgment. However, God had always kept God's part of the covenant and had never abandoned Israel.

I cannot think of anything my children (now adults) could do that would make me disown them or cast them out. If that is true for me, how much more would it be true for God. That is the way God has been with Israel; and now, Jeremiah says, in a new covenant God would give grace to the people so that they would want to obey, to be faithful, and to live as God's people.

God has always forgiven God's people. Forgiveness is nothing new. However, there is a sense in which this was a new time, when God would give a covenant that the people would not break.

Christians have looked at Jeremiah's words about a new covenant as a lens through which to understand Jesus. We connect Jeremiah's words to Jesus' words at the Last Supper about the new covenant in his blood and celebrate that new covenant when we participate in the Eucharist.

First, however, we have to remember that our interpretation is not what Jeremiah meant by the new covenant. He meant that God was entering into a new covenant with the people of Israel. We need to understand and appreciate that historical meaning before we add the layer of Christian interpretation to it.

Second, after we add that layer of interpretation, we need to remember that our interpretation in no way invalidates Jeremiah's understanding. God is still the God of Israel as well as of the church, and God has a covenant with Israel as well as with the church. God has never revoked that covenant, and Christian faith has deep roots in the covenants with Israel. God has indeed done a new thing in Jesus Christ, but the new means a great deal more when we recognize that it rests on the old.

What matters most is God's power of renewal. God does not abandon Israel and does not abandon us. God renews relationship when we fail and gives us new hearts and the desire to live God's way.

What does it mean to you to say that God's law will be written on your heart? How does this insight relate to your capacity to "start over" in your journey of faith?

JESUS AS HIGH PRIEST
HEBREWS 5:5-10

We recently spent time with two other couples with whom we have been friends for 50 years. All of us have a record of accomplishment in our chosen fields, and we also have felt good about our children and how they have thrived as adults.

However, as we talked about all the new things we have done over the years and how we have had accomplishments that our parents never dreamed of, we agreed on one thing. If it had not been for the solid family backgrounds from which we came, we would not have been the people we are or accomplished the things we have. Our parents taught us values and skills that have made all the difference in our lives. Without that foundation, the new things that we encountered would not have meant so much.

I believe that the men and women in the early church must have had some of the same kinds of feelings. Without what went before in their family of faith, they would never have appreciated the saving act of God in Jesus Christ.

The writer of Hebrews is one who was rooted in the traditions of God's covenant with Israel. In Hebrews 5:4, the writer mentions Aaron, the brother of Moses and the first high priest of Israel's faith. The writer says Aaron and Christ were called to the priesthood by God. Their calling was to glorify God, to represent God to Israel and the church—to Israel and the church to God. Israel's high priests must offer sacrifice for their own sins and for the sins of the people. Jesus was obedient and offered himself as the perfect sacrifice for all eternity.

When we read verse 5 and see the words "Son" and "begotten," we may recall the Nicene Creed, which spells out the relationship between the Father and the Son in the Trinity. This is not what the writer of Hebrews meant. Rather, he was quoting Psalm 2:7. There the words about sonship and begetting mean that God had appointed or designated Israel's king as God's Son. The writer of Hebrews made the same point by using the quotation. The key is what God has done. The method is sonship and kingship. This is an important point for the Christology of Hebrews.

Immediately following, and linked directly to Psalm 2:7, there is a quotation from Psalm 110:4, which suggests that Christ is a priest forever, like Melchizedek. Melchizedek is one of those mysterious figures who appears only once in the narrative parts of the Old Testament.

In the story of Abraham going after the raiders who had devastated his neighborhood and kidnapped Lot, among others, we find that when Abraham returned victorious, he was met by Melchizedek, the king of Salem. Then Abraham offered tithes to Melchizedek (Genesis 14:17-20). As a result of this brief mention, the biblical tradition has seen Melchizedek as king and high priest.

Quoting these two psalms brings together two ways of talking about Christ: kingship and priesthood. Psalm 2:7 serves to point out Christ as king; Psalm 110:7 names him as priest, just as Melchizedek was king and priest. Both are important images for the Christology of Hebrews.

After stressing that Jesus is of God, the writer turns to speaking of him as one of the people. This is the meaning of the phrase "in the days of his flesh" (Hebrews 5:7). This is the word about the Incarnation: Jesus was truly human as well as truly God. In Jesus of Nazareth, the Word of God, the Second Person of the Trinity, took on flesh and lived on earth as a full human being. As a human being, Jesus prayed "with loud cries and tears" (verse 7). This may be an allusion to Jesus' prayer in the garden of Gethsemane, asking that the cup of death could pass from him.

If Jesus was God, then why didn't God hear his prayer in Gethsemane and save him from the kind of death he suffered? The fact is that God did hear Jesus' prayer, but Jesus still suffered. We have the same experience in prayer, that is, we believe God hears our prayers and yet we still suffer pain and disappointment. We are reminded that Jesus is one of us in being fully human because we share the same kinds of experience in prayer.

Being God's Son did not exempt Jesus from learning, obedience, or suffering. The three terms are linked in a way much more profound than "learning from our mistakes." Rather the point is that obedience does not automatically lead to happiness; nor does suffering indicate that one has been disobedient. Jesus was obedient, and he chose to suffer. In contrast to the high priests, he offered himself as the perfect, single sacrifice for sins (10:12). As the "great high priest" (4:14), he is able to intercede for us and he is "the source of eternal salvation for all who obey him" (5:9).

Verse 9 suggests that Jesus was made perfect through suffering.

This was not an act of moral achievement. Rather, *perfection* here means "complete" or "finished." Through suffering, Jesus' identity as high priest was completed. He completed the task for which he came into the world, namely our salvation.

What does the understanding of Jesus as "great high priest" say to you about traditions in a family of faith? What does it mean to your life of faith that Jesus is "the source of eternal salvation for all who obey him"?

NOW IS THE HOUR
JOHN 12:20-33

We lived about two hours from St. Louis; and, every once in a while, we would have to go into the city to shop for clothes we could not find in our little town. One year we went to the old St. Louis Theater to see a double feature. One of the movies was *High Noon*, starring Gary Cooper as a marshal. The title came from the time the train arrived at the station. The train was carrying a man whom Gary Cooper, as marshal, had sent to prison, and who had vowed to come back and kill him.

Part of the tension in the movie was the clock ticking down to the hour of noon. The hour was when something significant would happen. Our Gospel text is about another hour. It was the "hour" for Jesus' glorification.

The Greeks wanted to "see" Jesus. They asked Philip, who told Andrew and the two of them to take the request to Jesus. In the beginning of Jesus' ministry,

Andrew askd Jesus about where he was staying, to which Jesus replied, "Come and see." Philip, also, invited a skeptical Nathanael to "come and see" (John 1:39).

Just as Philip and Andrew were the first to become Jesus' disciples, now there was a connection between them and the first Gentile disciples. This was a glimpse of the future—the mission to the Gentiles and their inclusion in all the promises of God. It pointed toward Jesus' ultimate goal: the salvation of the whole world.

This glimpse of the future also marked the beginning of Jesus' hour. This "hour," in the fourth Gospel, was the turning point toward Jesus' glorification, which would be accomplished through the Crucifixion, Resurrection, and Ascension. Through this glorification, God's promises to God's people would come true; but that future would require Jesus' death.

Jesus began teaching about the meaning of his death with a parable from agriculture. A grain of wheat has to be put into the ground and die before it can bear fruit. Seeds decay so that they can sprout and make new plants, which in turn produce many grains of wheat. The contrast between remaining solitary and bearing much fruit is important.

In John's Gospel, fruit is Jesus' metaphor for the life of the community. So this parable shows that the saving power of his death lives in the community that comes together because of his death.

In John 12:25, we find one of the sayings of Jesus that is found elsewhere in the other Gospels: "Those who love their life lose it, and those who hate their life in this world will keep it for eternal life." Now here is the kicker: To love one's life is the opposite of Jesus' own action. To cling selfishly to our own desires and hopes, our own "life," is to be outside of the community, which is shaped by Jesus' gift of his life. On the other hand, to hate one's life in the world is to pledge allegiance to Jesus and to receive his gift of eternal life.

We find examples of this in the lives of men and women throughout the church. Saint Augustine began his career as a student of Manichaeism and Neo-Platonism and as a teacher. Later, after his conversion to Christianity, he became the bishop of the church in Hippo, in North Africa. Albert Schweitzer began his career as a scholar and an internationally known organist, but he spent most of his life as a medical missionary in Africa. Both gained life because they were willing to give up their lives.

Verse 26 holds a condition and a promise. The condition is following Jesus in a life of service—to love as he loves and to serve as he serves. For many, that will mean serving without getting much credit for it. Whether it is washing dishes in the community soup kitchen or teaching children in the church, whether it is the person who comes to the church every week and takes care of the flowerbeds or the person who delivers Meals on Wheels, there may not be much glory or thanks.

However, the life of service is exactly what Jesus calls us to. We may not be called literally to die for Jesus' sake, but we may be called to die to our hopes for recognition and credit in this world. That is the condition.

The promise is that when we follow Jesus to his death, we also follow him through his death to glorification. Actually, there are two related promises. The first is that wherever Jesus is, his servant will be there also. The second is that God will honor whoever serves Jesus. Think of that! When we serve others, we serve Jesus as well. Although the world may not honor us for our service—in fact, the world may scoff at us because we give up something in order to serve—God will honor us.

Which leads to an obvious question: Which would you rather have—honor from the world or honor from God? The answer is not always easy. We want honor from God, but we also would like honor from the world. We have to work hard to keep our focus on following Jesus in a life of service.

Jesus did not go cheerfully to the cross, as verses 27-28 remind us. The writer of the Gospel says he was "troubled" about the hour before him. Well, who wouldn't be? This is yet another example of Jesus' humanity. He was troubled at the thought of the cruel torture involved in death by crucifixion. However, he asked rhetorically, "Should I pray to be saved from this hour?" Then he answered his own question. "This hour is the reason I came into the world. So the only prayer worth praying is 'Father, glorify your name.'"

A voice came from heaven affirming that was the only prayer worth praying: "I have glorified it and I will glorify it again." The voice affirmed what God had already done in Jesus and what God would do in the events of the Crucifixion, Resurrection, and Ascension.

The crowd thought it had thundered or that an angel had spoken. Thunder was a common symbol for the voice of God, and angels were God's messengers. The crowed recognized they were witnessing a revelation of God. What they missed was the presence of God in Jesus. When we gather in worship, when we hear the preaching of the Word, when we hear the great music of the ages in the playing of the organ and the singing of hymns, when we partake of the sacrament, do we know we are in the presence of God? What do we miss?

Finally, Jesus said that when he was lifted up, he would draw all humanity to himself. "Lifting up from the earth" could be a clear reference to the Crucifixion, as we saw in an earlier session about Moses and the serpent. It could also mean the final glorification in the Ascension, the return to the Father. It could mean both. In any case, the message is clear. The Crucifixion-Resurrection-Ascension is the great salvation event. People will be drawn to Jesus and to the community of faith that lives in his name, because of this lifting up.

The will of God is that all persons should be saved. Whether we are saved depends on our response to Jesus and to his being lifted up in this hour of pain and glory.

How do you respond to the parable about the grain of wheat? What does it mean to you to lose your life in order to gain your life?

Humiliation and Vindication

Scriptures for Lent:
The Sixth Sunday
Isaiah 50:4-9a
Philippians 2:5-11
Mark 15

"How humiliating!" We have all heard those words at one time or another. We have even felt the power of those words, because we have been humiliated. Whether it was being taunted by the schoolyard bully, dressed down by a professor in front of an entire classroom, or fired from a job for reasons that made no sense, we all know what it is like to be humiliated.

How much worse, then, must it be to find oneself humiliated because of one's faith, to be humiliated because we tried to be faithful to God? Today's Scripture passages are about that kind of humiliation and the vindication that comes to those who are faithful to God.

Isaiah 50:4-9a is about God's servant, that mysterious person mentioned as an example for his people. The servant had been faithful, trying to bring God's word to a reluctant people. All he received in return was humiliation, but he also knew the strengthening presence of God.

Philippians 2:5-11 is a great hymn from the earliest days of the church. It sings of the preexistent glory of Christ, the humiliation that comes from self-giving to the world through the Incarnation and the obedience unto death. Then it sings of the glory of the risen and ascended Christ.

Mark 15 reminds us of the ultimate humiliation. Jesus was crucified, with all the torture and agony that form of death involves. He was publicly humiliated, scoffed at by the priests and the passersby, and left almost alone to die. The first sign of his ultimate vindication comes in the words of the centurion in charge of the death squad: "Surely this was the Son of God!"

As we prepare for Holy Week, let us keep ourselves open to the strengthening presence of God, even during the humiliation that Jesus the Christ bore for our sakes, so that we will be ready for the full glory of Easter.

CONFIDENCE IN THE FACE
OF SUFFERING
ISAIAH 50:4-9a

Modern preachers—as well as laity—could be envious of the servant of God because of the gifts God had given him. The first is that he knew the right thing to say at the right time, something we all need. This was because of his personal spiritual relationship with God, a gift of grace. Because of that gift, he knew how to "sustain the weary with a word" (Isaiah 50:4). That was a tremendous gift for his time.

The prophet and his people were in exile in Babylon. They had been defeated militarily. They had been torn from their homes and had had to adjust to living in a strange land. Above all, they were disheartened and dispirited and needed to find hope for their lives. They needed a word to sustain them.

With some variations, that sounds much like the situation of many people in many parts of the world today. Whether it is because of natural disasters such as earthquakes and tsunamis, war, loss of loved ones or of jobs or homes, people today need to hear a word that sustains them. Speaking that word is also the task of a servant church, just as it was for the servant, who was gifted with words to sustain his people.

When the end of the exile seemed near and the people began to look ahead to the struggles of rebuilding their homeland, they needed a strong word to sustain them. The prophet said it was the word of God that came to him morning by morning and the gift that allowed him to hear the word. In Hebrew thought, the ear was the bodily organ by which one responded to the revelation of God. It was also the open door to discipleship. "To hear is to obey" was not an empty phrase for the Israelites. Revelation always calls for obedient response. God works on a vast scale but also in the inward heart.

Following the Word of God has never been easy. The servant had to deal with disbelief, distrust, and even active persecution from opponents among his own people. The people addressed here are the Israelites who had been unfaithful, who had lost hope, and who had given up their roots in the covenant community (verses 5-6).

The servant had tried to be faithful. He stood up for God and for what God wanted from him, even in the face of all the ugly responses he received. "I gave my back to those who struck me" (verse 6), the servant said. Flogging is an awful punishment, designed to lay open the skin and muscles of the back down to the bone. However, equally as horrible was that the servant gave his "cheeks to those who pulled out the beard."

I cannot imagine sitting still and taking it while someone pulled out my beard, perhaps a few hairs at a time. Note that he did not say, "cut my beard"; he said, "pulled out the beard." Ouch! In addition to causing physical pain, pulling out the beard was a strong insult. This was literally adding insult to injury. Moreover, the servant did not hide from insult and spitting.

In the face of all this, the prophetic servant found strength and help from God. Because God helped him, he had not been disgraced. All that he had suffered had not defeated him nor made him seem as nothing in public opinion. Rather he had been given strength so that he was able to say, "I have set my face like flint" (verse 7), that is, to stand firm in the face of all the abuse poured out on him. Even though he had been publicly insulted and shamed in the sight of men, he knew that he would not be put to shame in the eyes of God, for he had been faithful.

The one who vindicated him was near. The servant had a sense of personal fellowship and communion with God. He also was convinced that God would defend his cause and he would be publicly vindicated soon.

Being faithful in hard times is one of the most difficult things we have to do. I was a brand-new preacher at the height of the civil rights era in the United States. I cannot imagine how people who were working for civil rights were able to face continued beatings, water cannons, and even the deaths of colleagues and friends. I am not sure I could have been that faithful. I wonder also how we can be faithful in today's world. What are some of the ways in which the world abuses us, in which we receive the metaphorical equivalents of pulling out the beard? How do we stay in the kitchen when the heat rises?

The answers bring us back to our relationship with God. The servant was convinced that if we take a stand for the right because it is right and because God wills it, we will be vindicated. I love the three rhetorical questions that the prophet asks in verses 8-10. They offer answers that in turn offer hope.

First question: Who will contend with me? It is almost a "come on, put up or shut up" kind of question. If you have something to say, let us get it out into the open. If you are against me, stand up and say so. It is an expression of confidence in the God who supported the servant within his situation of distress.

Second question: The Lord helped the servant so who could declare him guilty? I think of Paul's statement in Romans 8:31: "If God is for us, who is against us?" Paul's words are much like what the prophet was saying. All those who were against him would wear out like that shirt hanging in the back of the closet for too many years. It is worn out and no longer any good. In fact, it has been back there so long the moths have eaten holes in it (Isaiah 50:9).

Third question: Who fears the Lord and listens to God's servant? The question points to hope. Isaiah 50:4-9a affirms that God gave the servant and the people of Israel what was needed to make it through the humiliation and abuse of tough times. God does the same for us today. Verse 9a, the actual end of the reading, summarizes the hope and help we need: "It is the Lord GOD who helps me."

How have you experienced confidence in God's support and presence? Was it during tough or humiliating times? What was it like for you?

FROM HUMILITY
TO EXALTATION
PHILIPPIANS 2:5-11

This passage from Paul's letter to the church at Philippi may be a hymn from the "childhood" of the church. It is highly poetic, and in it we find a remarkable movement from divinity to self-emptying humility and death to exaltation. This passage deals with the Incarnation and the ultimate exaltation of Christ. We see in these verses an echo of the same themes that we have already seen in the passage from Isaiah: humiliation and vindication.

The verses raise questions about the preexistence of Christ. He was in the form of God. There is nothing here about the nature of that preexistence, simply that it was. Think what he could have done with that power. However, being God, he did not consider that status as something to be exploited. Rather, he emptied himself, or made himself nothing compared to the glory that was his by right, and became human. Verse 7 says that he took on the status of a slave! The term emphasizes the contrast between his preexistent nature with the lowliness of his human nature.

Being found as a human, he became obedient to all the limitations of humanity, up to and including death. Verses 7-8 express two great doctrines. The first is the Incarnation, the coming of the Son of God into the world in human flesh so that he might bring about the salvation of the world. The second is the Crucifixion event, which Christians of all generations have seen as the climactic act of salvation.

As we celebrate Palm Sunday, we do so in the shadow of the cross that loomed before Jesus, even as he entered Jerusalem. Most of us would rather skip from the triumphant parade of Palm Sunday to the glories of Easter without thinking too much about what comes between; but we need to remember the cross, the ultimate in humiliation and suffering. Jesus the Christ became obedient to that death, and we dare not pass over it lightly.

When these verses talk about the form, or the nature, of God, it is language about what God does. What God does is to take on human flesh, emptying God's self for the sake of the world. If we want to see God's glory, we look at Christ's emptying and obedience to death. We may learn that God expects similar actions from us. To be a follower of Jesus is not a quest for status or power. It is not about getting ahead or about having the symbols of success in the world. To give ourselves for the good of others is to follow the example of God-in-Christ.

Then comes the "therefore" that marks the further action of God, who responds to the humiliation of Christ. Notice all the superlatives in these short verses: Jesus is given the name above every name; every knee shall bow to him; every tongue will confess him Lord; he is exalted to the highest status.

Names are important. Perhaps you have heard the saying about giving a dog a bad name, which means that we treat another on the basis of the reputation that goes with the name. We talk about winning a name for ourselves, which means gaining status and power.

What God did for Jesus was a powerful reversal from humility to exaltation. Jesus was given the name above every name, that is, the name of God. In Hebrew tradition, the name of God was never spoken. Instead, the phrase *the Lord* was used as a substitute. So when verse 11 proclaims that Jesus is Lord, it is saying that the one who bore the humiliation now carries the wonder and glory of God.

In Philippi, where the worship of the emperor was important as a sign of patriotism, saying that Jesus is Lord would have been a real challenge to political realities. In a time and place when "patriotism" is considered a high value, when loyalty to political party or political ideology is considered to be more important than the good of the country, this hymn comes as a reminder that it is Jesus Christ who is Lord, not the "gods" of this world.

Verse 10 says, "At the name of Jesus every knee should bend." In societies where kneeling to show respect is a common practice, one kneels only to superiors. There is a clearly understood structure of who kneels to whom. So when every knee bends, that means no one is greater than Jesus. The one who gave himself in humiliation has come into his Kingdom and all shall bend the knee to him.

The exaltation of Jesus Christ is for the glory of God. Whoever honors Jesus glorifies God, because Jesus is the one who "is in the form of God" and reflects God's glory.

What feelings or thoughts occur to you about Jesus Christ's willing obedience and humility and his ultimate exaltation? In what ways can you follow the example of his self-giving in your life of faith?

GOD IS PRESENT
MARK 15

One year, when I was a young preacher, I was asked to preach at the union Good Friday service in our village. How do you say something new about the crucifixion of Jesus? I struggled with that for a couple of weeks and then hit on this strategy. I did not preach. What I did was read the account of the Crucifixion of a slave/rebel from Howard Fast's novel *Spartacus.* Then I read Mark 15. Finally, I repeated the closing words of the two accounts. In the novel, the Roman soldier says, "God, I'm thirsty." In Mark, the centurion says, "Truly this man was God's Son!" I closed by suggesting that we had the choice of two responses, laid before us by the Roman soldiers.

That is sort of where we are today. It is not Good Friday; but even on Palm Sunday, we know that Good Friday is coming. The cross looms before us, and we have to get past it before we can come to Easter.

This is a long selection of Scripture; and we will not attempt to discuss the details, which would take us far beyond the limits of our space here. Rather, we will look at some of the issues that the text raises for us today.

First is "who was responsible for the death of Jesus?" Historically, the Jewish authorities and Pilate, representing the power of Rome, bear responsibility. It is ironic that Barabbas was guilty of the very crimes with which Jesus was charged. It is even more ironic, for me at least, that the name *Barabbas* means "son of the father." The real Son of the Father died so that the false son could go free!

Responsibility rests on those who participate in the deceit and power politics that allow innocent persons to be sacrificed. In the trial of Jesus, that meant those who were more interested in their own position, ideologies, or power than in the truth or the greater good. In our day, it could mean those who are more concerned with power and ideology than with the good of the weak and marginalized in our society.

The Roman soldiers mocked Jesus and beat him, which reminds us that depersonalizing victims increases violence in any society. The publicized plight of one person or one family catches the attention and sympathy of society and leads to an outpouring of help. The same plight of thousands of people does not catch the attention or rouse the support of society for those thousands.

Perhaps worse, the authorities in Jesus' day did not care who was innocent and who was guilty. They were perfectly willing to sacrifice the innocent and free the guilty if it suited their ends and desires for power.

The Crucifixion was the ultimate humiliation of Jesus. Crucifixion was one of the most painful of all deaths. In addition to the pain and the sure knowledge of coming death, there was the humiliation of being exposed to the crowds passing by. The place of crucifixion was just outside the city on one of the busy roads leading to the gates. Everyone going into or out of the city could see the torture and humiliation of those who were being crucified. The crowds mocked those who were dying, and the authorities called on Jesus to save himself by coming down from the cross (verse 30). Their intent was clearly to remind him of just how powerless he was.

Jesus was offered sour wine but refused it. He would die in full possession of his powers. The soldiers casting lots for his clothes echoes Psalm 22, which is used several times in the account of the Crucifixion. Jesus prayed the opening words of the psalm as he approached death. Mark may have intended this to mean that Jesus felt abandoned by God. If so, he was identifying fully with suffering humanity. The incarnation of the Son of God means that he became fully human and, as the Epistle reading suggests, became obedient even unto death.

The sign on Jesus' cross read, "The King of the Jews"; and it indicated the crime of insurrection. Yet, a Roman centurion saw how Jesus died and said, "Truly this man was God's Son" (verse 39). The oppressor, the enemy, was forced to admit that the oppressed one is superior—even to the power of Rome.

CALL HIM SAVIOR

The chapter ends with the story of those who cared for the dead body of Jesus. Joseph of Arimathea buried the body in a nearby tomb. The women watched and "saw where the body was laid." They were faithful women who had followed Jesus from Galilee and stood by him while he was dying. Why are they important to the story? They were the witnesses whose presence at the burial points to the completion of the story. These two and Salome would return to the tomb after the sabbath to anoint the body and find that it was gone.

The Crucifixion has to be seen in context, as part of a greater whole. It is one step in a saving journey that also includes the Resurrection and the Ascension. As we celebrate Holy Week on Friday, it seems that death is triumphant, that evil has won, that sin has overpowered even God's love. Yet throughout the horror of the Crucifixion, God is present. God could have sent the legions of angels to overcome the power of Rome. Instead God chose suffering in order to identify fully with the realities of human life. The cross iden-tifies the power and presence of God with the weak in the world.

We continue to find God in the sufferings of the present. In the wake of the disasters of September 11, 2001, people were asking, "Where is God?" Where was God? God was with the firemen and other responders rushing up the stairs of the towers, risking their lives in the attempt to save others. God was with those passengers on the plane, knowing they were facing certain death and calling their loved ones to reassure them. Yes, God was with the hijackers who were crashing the planes into the towers. God was with them all, just as God was with the one who was crucified for us.

The Roman centurion recognized God's triumph at the Crucifixion. At the moment in which it seemed that good had been defeated and that death was victorious, he confessed Jesus as the Son of God.

How have you experienced or sensed the presence of God during times of suffering, loss, or humiliation? What does the cross suggest to you about the nature of God?

Witness to the Savior

Scriptures for Easter:
Acts 10:34-43
1 Corinthians 15:1-11
Mark 16:1-8

I have vivid memories of waking up on Easter Sunday to the sounds of my parents (and my aunt and uncle, who were visiting for the weekend) trying to quietly get out the door for the sunrise service. I always got right up and dressed so I could go with them. Easter sunrise service was a big deal in our little town. Even when I had no idea what it all meant, I felt something and wanted to be part of Easter in every way I could.

On the way home from the service, we stopped and bought the Sunday paper. The Sunday magazine always had a picture of Easter lilies on the cover. Outside, there were signs of spring. Daffodils were blooming, there was fresh grass, and the trees were putting out leaf buds. New life was all around. It was easy to think about resurrection and new life in that setting, even though I was too young to have any idea what resurrection meant.

Since those days, I have thought a lot about the way we celebrate Easter. We do think in terms of new life, flowers, lambs, baby chickens, and so on. However, in the Southern Hemisphere, when Christians celebrate Easter, it is autumn. The earth begins its annual sinking back into rest for the winter, and the atmosphere is more like death than life. I wonder a lot about how we would celebrate Easter in that setting. How does one celebrate new life in the dying of the year?

The Resurrection, however, is about more than symbols of newness in the world around us. It is about newness come into a world of death and despair. It is about a new world order because Christ has been raised out of death. Sin and death and evil have been overcome in the Crucifixion, Resurrection, and Ascension of Jesus. God has made a new world. We do not yet see that new world in all its fullness, but it has begun. The question is, What do we do with Easter? What difference does it make in our lives?

Today's readings offer insights about what the Resurrection meant to the early church and what it can mean to us. They also offer insights about what God has done in Jesus Christ and why, as the title of our study proclaims, we CALL HIM SAVIOR.

Acts 10:34-43 records Peter's sermon to the centurion Cornelius and his household. In it, Peter proclaims the power of the risen Christ to bring new life and salvation to all people. First Corinthians 15:1-11 proclaims God's saving work through Jesus Christ and supports the proclamation with a list of Resurrection appearances of Christ and an affirmation of God's grace at work in the lives of believers.

Mark 16:1-8 tells the story of the women finding the empty tomb and hearing the news from a man in white that Jesus had been raised. All three call for a response to God's mighty act of salvation through the resurrection of Jesus Christ.

NEW LIFE FOR THE OUTSIDERS
ACTS 10:34-43

We attend a small urban church. It is a church for outsiders: those who have not found a home in other churches, where we feed the hungry twice a week, find homeless people sleeping on the porch of the church, and until recently had drug dealers operating on our corner. We invite all those people to become part of our fellowship.

Beyond that, we are a Reconciling Congregation; and many of our members have been outsiders because their previous churches did not welcome them after they "came out" as gay or lesbian. Many of them are wounded people. Our congregation is wounded because of the wounds of our people, and we try to support one another in the search for God's love and the power of new life.

Peter preached a similar message to Cornelius and his household. Before the sermon, we learn that Cornelius was a centurion in the Roman army, he feared God, gave alms, and prayed (Acts 10:1-2). He was a Gentile and thus an outsider to Judaism even though he was sympathetic to the faith. God spoke to him and told him to send men to Joppa (verse 5).

The narrative continues with an account of God's vision to Peter that challenged laws in Leviticus about clean and unclean foods and declared, "What God has made clean, you must not call profane" (verse 15). Peter was a little slow; but when that happened three times, he caught on that God was calling him to welcome outsiders.

In verses 34-43, Peter offers his new insights about God's salvation. Gentiles, outsiders, are welcome because of what God has done through Jesus Christ. His message is about the impartial love of God for all people. Before this experience, Peter had been doing what many good church people do even today—showing partiality.

Peter gave essential details about the life and teachings of Jesus. As the climax of his sermon, he said that Jesus was put to death by hanging him on a tree. "God raised him on the third day and allowed him to appear" to the disciples (verses 40-41). As a result, Peter said, "he commanded us to preach to the people . . . everyone who believes in him receives forgiveness of sins through his name" (verses 42, 43). God's mighty acts through Jesus Christ are intended for the good of all people, even for outsiders. God is impartial with God's salvation.

Peter did catch on, and he defended his new understanding in the church at Jerusalem (Chapter 11). They did not like the idea of Peter preaching to outsiders, much less baptizing them and inviting them into the church. Peter retold the events, acknowledged the presence of the Holy Spirit upon them, and said, "If then God gave them the same gift that he gave us when we believed in the Lord Jesus Christ, who was I that I could hinder God?" (11:17). God, speaking through the Spirit, told him there was a new day. The "unclean" were clean in God's sight, and the outsiders were invited to the table along with the insiders.

Peter's words raise a question for us: Do we hinder God? The Holy Spirit is continually leading the church into new worlds, and God's poking us may come through what goes on in the life around us. Peter's experience reminds us that we learn about God's will from God rather than entirely from our own insights. God does not sit back and watch but actively communicates over time what God's will is. We often learn that through "aha" experiences—maybe a whole chain of

them before we finally catch on to what God is trying to say to us.

Often we Christians believe that we are a chosen people, and that belief sometimes causes us to think that those who are different from us or who disagree with us are not chosen by God. We often do not like the idea of welcoming outsiders into the church and treating them as God's beloved children. We put labels on those outsiders as a way to keep them as far away as possible. God calls us—as well as Peter and the church at Jerusalem—to a renewed understanding of God's impartial love. God acts to save us, to transform us through Jesus Christ and the living power of his resurrection.

Who are the "outsiders" in your community? How might you open your heart and mind to a new understanding of God's love for these outsiders? What can you do to put this renewed understanding to work in your daily life?

WITNESSES TO THE FAITH
1 CORINTHIANS 15:1-11

I was blessed by growing up in the church. Before I started to school, I had learned many of the basic stories of the Bible. Mrs. Whitesell was important to me. She was committed to passing on to a new generation the biblical foundations of the faith. So I learned about Abraham and his descendants, Moses and Joshua, David and Goliath, and Elijah and Elisha. Above all, I learned about Jesus. The teachers I had in

Sunday school in later years continued the tradition. We learned more about the Bible itself in addition to the stories. We memorized verses and the order of the books in the Bible.

As we grew older, we learned more about how the faith applied to our lives. We were allowed to ask questions and discuss possibilities, not always a common practice in those days, and I will be forever grateful. Maybe even more important, we learned from the significant adults in our lives what it meant to live as Christian disciples in a world that was changing rapidly. We learned the good news and how to practice it in our lives by word and by example.

In 1 Corinthians 15:1-11, Paul reminds the church about the good news of the Resurrection and how it works in the lives of believers. First, he reminded them of the gospel as they had received it from him. They "stand" and "are being saved" by this good news (verses 1-2). Second, he mentioned the witnesses to the truth of what he was saying. Finally, he gave a personal testimony about his relationship to the gospel and to God's grace working through him.

Verses 3-4 give the essence of the gospel message. It is a simple message: (1) Christ died for our sins. (2) He was buried. (3) He was raised on the third day. The verb *raised* in the Greek is what is called a "divine passive," that is, it shows that it was God who did the raising. That is the foundational belief. It is like the statement of faith in the Eucharistic ritual, "Christ has died. Christ is risen. Christ will come again." That is it—

the faith in a nutshell. You could put that on a bumper sticker, and everyone who read it would know the message.

Paul gives a list of witnesses in verses 5-8. It is an interesting list. First, there is Cephas (Peter), then the Twelve. We have accounts of these appearances by Luke and John, and by implication in Matthew. Paul's list is the only record we have of the appearance to the 500 men and women at once, but Paul was sure that most of them were still alive and would be good witnesses to the risen Lord. Jesus appeared to James, Paul said.

Then there is the note of a final appearance to all the apostles. This could be the appearance recorded in Luke and again in Acts of the appearance to the apostles at the time of the ascension. That is a fairly significant number of witnesses and does not even count the women at the empty tomb, the disciples on the road to Emmaus, or the lakeside appearance recorded in John.

Paul placed his own experience of the risen Christ in the context of the previous appearances. As he did so, he established common ties in faith to the church at Corinth and to us. He was a witness and a model for the good news of God's salvation through Jesus Christ.

First, Paul said, he was not fit to be an apostle because he persecuted the church. Then he reminded the Corinthians that he "worked harder than any of [the other apostles]" (verse 10). This is one of those exaggerated statements that Paul loved to make in order to drive a point home. Here his point was not so much self-aggrandizement as it was an indication of God's grace. It was not his hard work that made the difference to the Corinthians' faith, but the grace of God that was working through him. So, he said, "whether it was I or [the other apostles]," it did not matter. "So we proclaim," Paul says, "and so you have come to believe" (verse 11).

Like Paul, we may consider ourselves unfit to witness to God's saving power in Jesus. We may have lived in such a way as to turn our backs on God. We often live as if God does not exist. We recognize our sinful nature; and, like Paul, we claim to be what we are because of the grace of God. The hymn "Amazing Grace" is as true for us as it was for its writer, John Newman. It reminds us of what we used to be, of what God did for us ("taught my heart to fear and grace my fears relieved"), of how God's grace stays with us and gives us life, and of how God promises life eternal. This is all the work of God, who sent his only Son into the world to share God's grace with us.

With that, let us go back to Mrs. Whitesell and all the other teachers and examples I had as a child and a teenager. They knew the old stories about the faith, they knew their place in those stories, and they helped me link my life into the stories. Like me, you have your fathers and mothers in the faith. They may have been your biological parents or teachers and leaders in the church, but you had them. You are indebted to them because they carried the faith from the past, from the pages of the Scriptures, and made it part of your life. They gave it to us and worked with the Spirit to shape our lives after the example of Christ.

The church is an endless line of faithful witnesses, receiving the message from those ahead of us and passing it on to those who come behind us. I have been the beneficiary of that endless line. I try to pass on the faith to those who come behind. You, like Paul, like the Corinthians, like me, have received the benefit of the good news of God's mighty act of salvation in Jesus Christ and of the ongoing grace of God at work in our lives.

Who were the witnesses of the good news of the Resurrection and of God's grace through Jesus Christ? What difference has their witness made in your life? How can you share the good news with others in your life?

WHAT DO WE DO WITH EASTER?
MARK 16:1-8

We were in New York City for a training session for leaders of boards of missions across the United States. We actually participated in all the training, but the best part of the event was when we had to explore the city and take in the shows. We got "two-fers" (two for the price of one) tickets to see *Jesus Christ, Superstar!* What a deal!

I saw the show with a preacher from a little county-seat church in north Missouri. The show was the one we had built our senior-high camp around the summer before —the life of Jesus. Well, the play was magnificent! The acting was great, the music was everything you would expect from Andrew Lloyd Webber, and the staging was incredible. We were on Broadway, but . . . I came away feeling so disappointed. I remember saying to my colleague, "They didn't know what to do with the Resurrection!"

We do not know what to do with the Resurrection, either, and we are in church! How could I expect that Broadway would know what to do with it?

As we read Mark, we can see that the first witnesses did not know what to do with the Resurrection, either. They had the advantage of being with Jesus when he told them he would rise again on the third day, and they still did not get it. Let us look at the story as Mark tells it.

The women were going to the tomb early on the morning after the sabbath. They were not going with any expectations of a resurrection. They were going to anoint the body with spices, to complete the work of preparation that there had not been time for on Friday.

They were not expecting anything miraculous to happen at all. Their major concern was who would roll the stone away from the entrance to the tomb. Remember that Jesus' burial took place in a cave where the body was laid out on a stone bench. Then a large stone was rolled across the entrance. Moving the stone would take at least several strong men, a task beyond the strength and ability of three women.

They found the tomb and discovered that the stone had already been rolled back. A little uneasy, they entered the tomb and discovered that Jesus' body was not there. Instead, on the bench where the body had been was a young man dressed in white. This was not what they had expected. Mark says they were alarmed! I imagine that is putting it mildly! Frightened, yes. Unsure, yes. Concerned, yes.

The young man told them not to be alarmed. Jesus, he said, had been raised. The grammar is important. Note the verb is passive. It does not say Jesus rose. It says that Jesus had been raised. This is a way of saying that God did it. What they saw was not just an empty tomb, but the evidence of a mighty act of God.

By itself, the empty tomb does not prove anything except that the tomb was empty. The tomb does not explain the act of God. The act of God explains the empty tomb. The tomb was empty because God had raised Jesus. In this mighty act of God, expressed in crucifixion and resurrection, death was overcome. What looked like the end on Friday proved to be a new beginning for all humanity on Sunday. The "place where they laid him" was empty because God had overcome death.

The young man then told them, "Go, tell his disciples and Peter that he is going ahead of you to Galilee; there you will see him, just as he told you" (verse 7). The response was a human reaction. The women fled from the tomb. This was not the joyful running to the disciples of Mary Magdalene in John's Gospel. This was terror. The world they had expected was suddenly turned upside down, and they did not know what to do with

CALL HIM SAVIOR

it. So they did nothing. They did not tell anyone, according to Mark, because they were afraid.

How do we react to Easter? We go to worship, but the church is full because people "come home" for Easter, to be with family on this holiday weekend. People who regularly attend church once or twice a month all come at the same time on Easter. Then there are those who almost never attend church but are there for Easter. It is the thing to do.

We sing "Christ the Lord Is Risen Today" and "Up From the Grave He Arose" and rejoice in the glory of the music and the excitement of all the people; but what do we do with the Resurrection? Is there a sense that God has done a great thing? Is there an awareness of new life and victory over death? How do we leave the church? Do we go away feeling a bit let down and not sure why? Is that because we did not hear the power and wonder of the Resurrection preached and sung or because we did not expect much in the first place. What do we do with the Resurrection? How will our lives be different this coming week because we have been to Easter?

In the midst of all these kinds of questions about Easter, the Resurrection, and our daily lives stands the proclamation: Christ died; Christ was raised; and as we recall in the title of this study, we CALL HIM SAVIOR. The witness of our readings tells us that through Christ, salvation is for all people and God's grace continues to work in our lives. It is a story worth telling.

What does the Resurrection mean to you? What difference does it make in your life?